Sins
of a
Mulatto
Outcast

Sins *of a* Mulatto Outcast

An 18-Hole Wayward Identity Quest: 2nd Edition

Round 1

By:

Robert Fouche'

ARPress
ILLUMINATING IDEAS
EMPOWERING VOICES

ARPress
45 Dan Road Suite 5
Canton MA 02021

Hotline: 1(888) 821-0229
Fax: 1(508) 545-7580

Ordering Information:

Quantity sales. Special discounts are available on quantity purchases by corporations, associations, and others. For details, contact the publisher at the address above.

Printed in the United States of America.

ISBN-13:   Paperback   979-8-89330-916-4
                eBook   979-8-89330-915-7

Library of Congress Control Number: 2024902463

To Allison, Christian, Ava, and
Elise.
I failed the 1st time, but I couldn't
give up!

Table of Contents

Introduction

For some reason, writing this book came easy to me. I was experiencing a midlife crisis while approaching forty. I realized the midpoint of life is not fifty years of age, but right now. I discovered I haven't really fulfilled the life I truly want, been to places I want to visit, or done the things that really matter with my wife. I was existing. I was not living. It seemed like everything I was doing was not rewarding. The everyday stress of corporate America, along with being a father, was beginning to devour my spirit. My marriage was failing, and I was not sure why. I was becoming inept socially because I felt like a failure. I decided to break myself down to find the root cause of my unhappiness instead of blaming others. I drifted away from the principles I was taught from my relatives and people who influenced me most growing up. I began to take inventory of my life and a storyline developed as I began to note events from my past. Though much of the content in this book is fiction, it is based on details from my childhood I feel I held onto for too long. The main character is a mirror image of me and the struggles I suffered growing up as a high yellow youth in a predominantly urban environment. I was always aware of my ethnicity growing up, but it was hard to get others to realize and understand. I am fortunate I was taught this at a young age, even though it took me a while to get a grasp on what I was seeing in the mirror.

In this book, I hope the reader will see prejudices do not only exist between two different races. All races have their internal preconceptions in some form or another. A person should be defined by the content of their character and not the color of their skin. This book should also bring awareness to how one's looks can be deceiving to those who are ignorant about the evolution of race in America. Homer's journey—the main character—inspires all to understand it is not where you start but where you finish. Most of us are afraid to start a journey because it does not conform to the acceptance of others. Sometimes, we must be willing to accept the criticism and follow our own path. Homer cannot be faulted for the hand he receives. However, he finds difficulties in learning to play the cards he has been dealt.

Golf is a piece of my life that keeps me sane. It is a game no one will conquer. You can only contain it for a short time. The ups and downs of playing the game of golf are the same as Homer's journey of emotions.

Memphis is the setting of the story. Memphis is a wonderful city but is tarnished by the racial violence of the sixties. Just like all urban areas, rough spots are sprinkled around the city. Memphis often gets a bad reputation from the media due to violence and drama reported to bring in viewers. However, what is portrayed on television only shows the actions of the minority in this city. For those who know Memphis well, most of us who grew up in the area have become extraordinary citizens. Memphis has produced doctors, lawyers, politicians, entrepreneurs, and entertainers. It is a shame leadership over the last few decades has prevented the metropolitan area from becoming a hotbed like Dallas, Nashville, or Atlanta. Due to limited opportunities, most of the talent produced here has moved to more prosperous areas where opportunities are abundant. Memphis a jewel and the only thing negative about this great city is the summer weather.

Hole 1 – The Practice Tee

Sitting in a hospital room the night before my infant daughter is to have open heart surgery, I begin to backtrack through my life, trying to piece together the confusion my wife and I are feeling. Both of us are jumping at the chance to trade places with our daughter who is lying helpless on the hospital bed. I sit up, thinking my baby is suffering because of the sins of my past. Most of our relatives and friends are commending me on being calm and strong during this difficult situation. I must show strength for my wife because she is a nervous wreck. To tell the truth, I am about to explode on the inside because the thought of my child being cut open is quite disconcerting. I am used to being calm in hectic circumstances and for some reason, I have this remarkable serenity everything will work itself out regarding my baby.

A conversation with my brother-in-law at Thanksgiving surfaces in my head. Sometime after dinner, the subject surfaces about how and where we grew up.

"You should never forget where you come from." He distinctly states.

Well, I disagree. I do not want to remember how I grew up because some things in my past bring back some painful memories. Growing up in the circumstances of my youth has left me wounded. Looking different forced me into a shell as a youth. Each time I think I am coming out of my comfort

1

zone, something happens to draw me back inside, forcing me to guard my emotions. I keep my feelings safeguarded because those I usually let in always seem to disappear. Some have even taken advantage of my emotional state, causing me to protect my feelings, rendering me nonchalant and detached. Some think I have an advantage because of my appearance, but to me it is a curse. Having constant struggles finding an identity is why I define being an outcast as a jinx. I want to know what my purpose is in this life. I feel I make bad decisions in trying to figure this out. Some of these decisions have been deplorable, causing the outcomes to become my sins.

Before I was married, I remember a verbal altercation between my wife and I, which forced me to enroll in anger management sessions. The therapist encouraged me to note things down from my past to help me understand where my anger issues were surfacing. The sessions occurred about nine years before my daughter was born. I did not take the therapist's advice at the time because I didn't want to relive the pain. Now, everything is beginning to spin out of control with my daughter's illness and my wife is appearing to have fallen out of love with me. My wife has painted a picture of me as an egomaniacal, controlling, sexual deviant. Even worse is she has my friends and family thinking it is true. I need to get everything on track before I fall back into the pool of anger and misery I recently surfaced from. I am working the best I can to make my wife happy and to provide a loving home for the kids. It's hard with our hectic schedules and my every move being scrutinized. While staring out the window of my daughter's hospital room, I pull out a pad from my travel bag and begin to notate my past.

Let me introduce myself. My name is Homer. The lifeline I am about to describe is hard to explain, because I am hard to define. I grew up differently than most kids. I thought

I was normal, but I kind of stood out amongst everyone. My neighborhood is all African American. I stand out because I am the lightest; well to be honest, I am considered the white kid in the crowd. I am tall, but skinny, with hazel eyes with very fair skin. If you do not know my background, I can easily camouflage myself within the Caucasian community. I look this way because of my parent's genetics. My father grew up in the deep rooted African American community of Orange Mound in the city of Memphis. His experiences growing up as a child were much deeper than mine. His tenure as a child took place during the Civil Rights Era of the 50s and 60s. Memphis represents the nucleus of racial divide in the South. My paternal grandfather is of Creole descent. Some of his forefathers could not take the segregation of the South. They feared being discriminated against because they are fair skinned, but people knew their true ethnic makeup. So, a group of my paternal ancestors decided to pack up and head west. Once settled, they assumed Caucasian identities in fear of the 'one drop rule' and lived as White Americans.

The one drop rule, referring to classification as Negro, if you have any African ancestry in your bloodline regardless of how far back in the generation. My grandfather's parents decided to stay in the Louisiana and Southern Mississippi area. Some migrated north, making their homes in Memphis up to Chicago and Detroit. They lived their lives as fair skinned African Americans while prospering in construction and other areas. My paternal grandmother is of Creole and Indian descent. Together, they produced three children you never can guess were legally classified as Negro.

My mother is a fair skinned beautiful woman, born to a stunning dark-skinned mother. My grandmother has perfect skin with beautiful long straight hair. Though my mother never told us, her biological father is a white man. I take it this gentleman was in the military and they conceived my mother during a brief affair. This affair would have not been approved during the 1940s because interracial relationships were illegal in Virginia. I never met him, and no one spoke of him. It does kind of make me wonder who he is, and if I have relatives I have never met.

My maternal grandmother met and married the greatest man I feel ever walked this earth. He raised my mother, and she referenced him as her father. My grandfather never made us feel we were not his biological grandkids. Every day during the summer, I waited for my grandfather on the side steps of the house or the back patio to come home from work. I always felt excited when he came home because everything just seemed different when he was around. He would talk to me about anything from cartoons, books, music, sex, girls, and stocks—basically everything a father should have been discussing with his son. What I like most is he does not hold his tongue. He might not think of himself as anything great, but he is immensely important to me. He always showed up at Christmastime and stayed with us for a week or two. As an elementary school kid, I would cry every time he departed to go back to Virginia. It wasn't so much the gifts, but his presence that made a difference.

My mother and father met at a Hampton University in the 60s. When they married, they decided to reside in my father's hometown of Memphis. The union of my mother and father produced my sister and me. Unfortunately, their union did not last long. My father was around when my sister was born, but he was having an affair with another woman while I was in the womb. As far as I know or can remember, my father wasn't around much until my sister and I were in our teenage years. Yeah, we saw him from time to time, but it was a "hi" and "bye" relationship without much meaningful conversation. To be fair to my father, I know there are two sides to every story. It just so happens I lived through one of those sides. We have yet to sit down as adults to discuss what drove a wedge in the relationship with my mother.

Once my sister and I got older, we realized why we were treated this way. It wasn't due to my father, but his new wife. We were never truly accepted by her. My father did what he must to keep his home happy. She knew he had us when she was courting him, so I never really understood why she treated us this way. She made us feel as though we always had to prove we were worthy to be his kids. She was quick to classify us as disgruntled and disobedient.

His marriage to my stepmother produced two half siblings. Of course, they look like us, but they grew up in a totally different environment than my sister and me. I never really researched how they are racially classified. Regardless of our relationship with my father and stepmother, we never treated our siblings any differently. Besides brother and sister arguments, we were pretty much a close-knit gang.

My sister and I suffered without a father present, but this is something I completely understand as a husband. I will do what my wife requests of me to keep the house happy. It is a painful memory I have as a child, but it gave me a blueprint to follow on parenting. The plan is basically to not follow his example. Regardless of how much I am pestered, I wouldn't allow anyone to deny me a relationship with my children. Once again, I give my father the benefit of the doubt because I know there are two sides to every story. My father paid child support, which is an essential part of the equation, but it does not substitute parenting, especially when trying to teach a son how to be a man. I felt as though he provided for us but didn't do much to protect us. Even though he was all too familiar with our circumstances, he never offered any advice or support on how to handle certain situations. My father did teach us some lessons, but I often wonder how things would have been if he was around full time.

It is funny how God works. No one will ever rationalize or develop a theory in full detail. It is something you must believe in to get a full understanding. The Lord knew I was lacking love in one area, but the awesome part of God is he fulfilled this void with the love given by my paternal grandmother and aunt. My sister and I spent almost every Friday night with my grandmother. My mother often went out partying. After spending the week battling two kids, she needed some R&R. I vividly remember my grandmother making popcorn in the old-style popper, and every year we watched *The Wizard of Oz* on its yearly run on television. My grandmother is very soft spoken but can get her point across with stern authority. She is still going strong at ninety-seven.

My paternal grandfather died when I was about three years old. I do not have many memories of him, but I remember staring at his photos wondering what he was like as a person. People often tell me I am the spitting image of my father, but I think I look like my grandfather. He was a tall, slender man, and we definitely resemble each other since I am now bald. I can tell by his pictures he was an extraordinary individual. A person people looked up to and admired. I hope this is the case because all the stories I hear pertain to his drinking habits; a genetic attribute I share with many family members.

I also spent time at my aunt's house growing up. This is another interesting union. My aunt looks like us, but my uncle has a dark complexion. They met in high school and eventually married. They produced three children where you would have to look twice to wonder if they were her kids. They all have a medium to dark complexion. You can hardly see any features my cousins inherited from my aunt. We spent a lot of time with my cousins growing up. They are like older brothers and sisters who helped us out a lot during our teenage years. They helped me embrace my ethnicity by teaching me not to be ashamed of how I look. I thought I was a white kid. I mean, I was looking in the mirror every day and seeing a Caucasian-looking individual staring back. I can remember all the looks we received when we were out together. People must have thought they kidnapped us. We were really an odd-looking bunch.

I learned a lot of lessons from my aunt and uncle. My uncle is a laid-back man, but a stern disciplinarian when you step out of line. I received my fair share of discipline from him. When I look back, it was all for my own good. Hell, as bad as I was, I needed it. Even though his discipline was harsh, he really was fair to all of us. He introduced me to the game of golf. My uncle is a pretty good golfer. He holds the most hole-in-one trophies I have ever seen. Once I got older, I realized he is one of the luckiest golfers ever. His miss hits are better than most guys' regular shots. We all need a little luck sometimes no matter what we are doing.

My aunt is more of the nurturing type. She made sure my sister and I were loved and pampered when we need it. I am pretty sure it is because she knows the full details of my mother and father's relationship. She wanted to make sure my sister and I got some type of love from my father's side of the family. I didn't care what the reason was, I just accepted it. I always felt safe and secure at my aunt and uncle's home. I hid in the pantry when my mom came to pick us up. I never wanted to leave. Every year, I tried to spend the night the day before Thanksgiving. My aunt put me to work crumbling up loaves of bread for the dressing and I enjoyed doing it. After spending time at school battling the neighborhood kids and the uncertainty of home, I just needed somewhere to go just to get away. Besides the golf course, her house is one of the few places where I can just be myself and feel no one can bother or hurt me.

The best of times from my early childhood came when we visited my mother's parents during the summer. My sister and I normally left for the summer after my junior golf tournaments and baseball schedule were complete. My grandmother is a schoolteacher, so we spent all our time with her during the day. My grandfather was one of the first African American Postmasters in the state of Virginia. I was able to go with him on occasions to watch the day in the life of the U.S. Postal Service. People of both races respected my grandfather. Since it is a small-town post office, my grandfather knew everyone and made an effort to converse with all the patrons, regardless of their nationality, when they visited.

Besides my mother, they have three other children, two uncles and an aunt. My aunt was born with a severe mental handicap, so we never saw her much because she stayed in a home to help manage her needs. One of my uncles is an ex-college football player and now a high school football coach who acts very strange. He is an introvert who lives in my grandparent's attic. We never have any meaningful conversations except when it comes to sports and some teasing of each other here and there. He always rides his bike late at night. He tells my sister and me he is going to Chicago and then turns around and comes back the next day. As we got older, we realized he is going to his girlfriend's house across town.

Then, there is my other uncle, who I consider one of my favorite people on Earth. He always took us places when he had time. He made us laugh until we couldn't breathe. To this day, he is still the same. I always look forward to his visits. I overheard a conversation between my grandfather and uncle where he comes out as gay. Of course, at the time, I didn't have a clue about the characterization of being a homosexual. During this era, homosexuality was shunned as an unacceptable lifestyle. Even though this isn't my lifestyle preference, I never think of him as anything other than my uncle. His sexuality never really mattered to me. He treats my sister and me like we are his own children. He always provides an ear to listen and a shoulder to cry on when needed.

My maternal grandmother has a troop of brothers and sisters, who have a squadron of children, who also have countless amounts of offspring. This is a big damn family. My grandmother sat in the house during the summer, watching her stories and drinking her rum. She got deeply involved in the storylines. When something bad happened, her face would frown and when something happy occurred, she smiled. I got a kick out of listening to her call the neighbors to discuss the storylines to these soaps during commercials.

On most evenings, as soon as the soaps were over and after dinner, she is off to her best friend's house. Her friend lived next door to her brother and they both had kids in our age range. We stayed out to the wee hours of the morning playing, singing, and doing whatever we wanted within reason. I still to this day cannot understand how she got us home every night, but we made it. The ride seemed like an eternity even though we only had to go a couple of miles. I love my grandmother. She is only one of a few people who are always honest with me regardless of the circumstance. My father once told me my grandmother can out drink most men. From what I noticed over the years, I agree with his assessment.

One evening, I got into a fight in the backyard with a kid who was bullying me because he thinks I am white. I am heading into the third grade and just like home; my sister and I are the lightest ones in the area. This kid makes a sexual gesture toward my sister, and I verbally attack him over it. After the tongue lashing, he knocks the hell out of me with a left blow to the face. I run into the house crying and my grandmother questions why.

"You go back out there and knock him on his hind parts. You never let anyone hit you like that." My grandmother stated sternly as she gently picked up my face, letting me know this is something I have to do.

I followed her instructions by punching the hell out of this kid. I don't think I won the fight because of my fighting skills. I think I won because the guy is shocked I retaliated this way. I am pretty sure if we fought again, he probably would lay me down with ease. My grandmother awoke an inner demon on that day. I never felt the sensation of confidence. This feeling lasted until a few incidents changed me.

Hole 2 – Identity Crisis

Memphis is broken down into sections of North, South, East, Downtown, Midtown, and Orange Mound. Each of these sections have their own neighborhoods most people recognize as their home subdivision. North Memphis' main areas are Frayser, Hollywood, and Hyde Park. Orange Mound was established in the early 1890s. It is the first neighborhood developed by African Americans in the United States. Up until the 1970s, Orange Mound was considered the Harlem of the south due to the concentration of black citizens in this one area of the city. The area flourished with cultural centers, minority owned business, and a mix of residences. Midtown is considered the cultural part of the city due to the architectural mansions, universities, and theaters. South Memphis is the largest section comprised of twenty-seven neighborhoods, which include Whitehaven, Westwood, Riverside, College Park, French Fort, and Pine Hill. Unfortunately, South Memphis is known as a hotbed for crime and the number of churches and liquor stores you may see on every main street corner. What most people do not realize is some of these neighborhoods consist of highly educated hard-working citizens and not the low-class hooligans the media portrays nightly.

I live in the Alcy section of South Memphis. I am fortunate enough to have my elementary school right up the street from my childhood home. Our house is in a nice middle-class section, but it is surrounded by a rough area of town. Being two minutes by foot from the house has its challenges. Even though most kids travel east to go home, I travel north. There are a lot of days when some of my classmates follow—better yet, chase—me to my house. I have a neighbor across the street from me who is always outside working on his RV or doing yard work. He scares the kids off when they get too close.

I am pretty smart, and the girls give me attention because I have long hair and green eyes. Some guys do not like the attention I receive or my appearance. Due to my appearance, the darker kids feel as though I am treated better than they are by the teachers. The truth is the teachers like me because I am a good student who takes school seriously. I never feel I am better than anyone. In actuality, I think I am inferior to them because I am the only one who looks the way I do at my school.

There is a stretch of woods dividing my street from the school about one hundred yards in length. On some days, I will get fifty yards from my doorstep before I get beat up. No one bothers my sister because they are trying to get her phone number to be her boyfriend. In the second grade, a guy who I think is my good friend falls under the circumstance of peer pressure and sucker punches me while I am getting a book from under my desk. The substitute teacher grabs me before I can do anything, but the way he hit me sort of discombobulates me a bit. The blow is hard but does not hurt. I am more emotionally wounded because we play together outside daily in our neighborhood. Of course, when others think I am a punching bag, they want to see how hard they can hit me. It gets to the point where these guys compete to see who can hit me the hardest to see my skin turn red.

Things change on the first day of school in the third grade. I am on my way home when a kid jumps in front of me and tries to prove how tough he is to his neighborhood friends. As he swings, I move to the side a bit, forcing him to miss. Thanks to my newfound confidence I found from my grandmother, I then grasp my new tin *Incredible Hulk* lunchbox and hit him in the temple area. As he is falling to the ground, another kid comes to his aid. I hit this kid with the other side of my lunchbox because I think he is coming for me. After a few seconds on the ground, they both get up and run off. Unfortunately for me, this occurs right in front of a teacher who is watching the parking lot during dismissal. I feel bad because in a moment of rage, I ruin the lunchbox I begged for all summer. I do not care that I just tried to bash two guys' heads in who were, in a sense, trying to bully me. I am punished by having to write five thousand times, '*I will not use my lunchbox as a weapon.*' I do not mind because I feel vindicated and free.

Unfortunately, this incident opens the floodgates to more bullying, terrorizing, and intimidation than normal. My friend, Grey, who sucker punched me in the second grade, is the worst culprit. He is trying to prove how tough he is to the kids who think we are uppity because we live in what is classified as the 'nice area.' Those of us who live in houses are considered middle class, while the kids who live in the apartments are considered lower class because of income. The class structure does not matter to me because I do not have money in my pocket anyway. Outside of these altercations, I meet some good folks in elementary school. Unfortunately, we have no clue how society and the ways of the urban street life will affect us once we get into our teenage years. In the third and fourth grade, the only things you care about are getting out of school, watching cartoons, playing outside, and learning about sports on TV.

One day during school, Grey catches me one on one in the restroom during a break at recess. While relieving myself at the urinal, Grey attempts to put me in a wrestling hold. The reason for attacking me is unknown. With me being so skinny and Grey being a bit overweight, he misjudges my size. For a skinny kid, I am quite strong for my build. As I spin out of his hold on me, Grey slips on the step leading to the urinals allowing me to drive his momentum into the stalls. A group of sixth graders walk into the restroom just as he hits the stalls. In their eyes, it appears as though I lift Grey off the ground and hip toss him into the stalls. While they are marveling over the event, this gives me enough time to slip out before Grey can retaliate. Thinking I have a sense of reprieve, I head back outside to recess, unknowing what is in store once school lets out.

As school dismisses for the day, rumors spread about how I manhandled Grey in the restroom. What is truly a huge sense of luck turns into a body slam into the wall, a wrestling hip toss into the stalls, and my favorite is a Popeye type uppercut, sending Grey flying backwards. Me being the person I am, I try to cool all the hype by telling the truth. However, I quickly realize people prefer rumors over facts. These rumors infuriate Grey. He wants revenge to remedy the situation as soon as possible. He cannot have the label of being beat up by the white kid as his reputation. Fortunately, I am halfway home, and it starts to rain by the time Grey can catch up with me.

Over the next few days, things are sort of quiet. I am in the gifted class and a small section of us separate from our regular class during school hours. During these classes, I can think and perform without worrying about being bullied or intimidated because of my skin tone. The kids in this class care less about my looks and only judge me based on my character. During downtime between schoolwork, I am thinking of ways to defend myself because I am not sure when Grey is going to attack. My best idea is to avoid Grey, but then I think about what my grandmother would think if I do so. I figure my best line of defense is to take him on whenever and wherever Grey wants to fight. The worst thing boosting my confidence is seeing *Rocky III* at the movies with my mother. After watching Rocky beat Clubber Lang, I feel I can fight Grey at any time.

A few weeks go by with no attacks. I know something strange is brewing because Grey and I play basketball a few times on the weekends at a neighbor's house. Some older kids, who think they are a dream team, try to use Grey and I like the team who always plays against the Harlem Globetrotters. This frustrates the both of us. It lights a fire because the one thing we both hate is to lose. This is where my competitive enthusiasm starts. We practice and eventually start giving these guys fits when we play. They always find a way to win in the end, but it is mostly due to their size rather than skill.

I think everything is okay between Grey and me until our last altercation in the restroom surfaces at lunch. Grey is playing the dozens with some kids in his class. Grey's opponent gets frustrated and brings up the incident. The insult puts Grey in check, only to bring up some old rage. After school dismisses, I must stay afterwards to rehearse for a program. After rehearsal, everyone is gone except for a few kids still waiting on their rides while horsing around. A girl's ride, who I have known since kindergarten, has not arrived yet. I stay with her, and we talk about the program and other things until her grandmother shows up. Her grandmother offers me a ride down the street, but I refuse because it is nice outside. Early spring in Memphis is usually one of the best times of the year regarding weather.

As I start my walk home, I wave at a few teachers who are leaving for the day. One of the teachers offers me a lift home, but once again I refuse because it is nice outside. Plus, it is a short distance. As I approach the stretch of woods dividing my street from the school, I feel something eerie. I can see my house, but it looks like it is two miles away in tunnel vision. I pass it off by enjoying the gentle breeze and I am not in a rush. My sister is already home, so I am by myself. I reach down to pick up a rusty penny when something hits me hard in the back of my leg, forcing me to fall. Then '*crack*', I feel something break across my back. It does not hurt or anything, but I am stunned by what is transpiring. Grey is attacking me with a rotten piece of wood. Apparently, Grey and some kids he is trying to impress were waiting to ambush me. Grey carries out the assault, while the other kids make sure I do not escape. I am able to get up, but a few punches to the head stun me a bit. When I try to run, the other kids cut off my path and shove me back towards Grey. One of the shoves eventually forces me to the ground.

In a blur, two gentlemen swoop in and break up everything. To my surprise, it is my neighbor, Slick, and his best friend, Hamp, who are college-age men. Slick is not a big guy but is bigger than us. Slick fits the description of a nerd. He does not have the ankle high pants or the pocket protector, but he is a little geeky. Slick is considered a genius because of his knowledge of computers and math, considering computers in the mid-80s were not as abundant and sophisticated as they are today. Hamp is what we call country strong. Hamp has worked for his father's tree service since he was six. Hamp is short in statue but has muscles everywhere, including in his neck. Hamp is kind of a social misfit but is a funny guy who does not pass up a chance to chase after a skirt.

Once they clear the chaos, Grey threatens Hamp by telling him this incident is none of their business. Before Grey can get the sentence out, Hamp hits him with an unforgettable body shot, which is still to this day one of the most ferocious punches I have ever seen someone absorb. Grey can only stand numb due to the force of the blow. Hell, he does not have a choice because Hamp has knocked the wind out of him. Once the other kids see the blow Grey receives, they scatter back towards the schoolyard because they fear one of them is next in line.

After getting my mindset back, trying to figure out what is going on, Grey's dad comes around the corner. Grey's dad is a Principal at another Elementary school nearby. He is on his way back to his school for a PTO meeting. Grey's dad pulls over to see what is happening. Slick and Hamp tell Grey's father what just occurred. Grey is still in shock from the punch from Hamp, so he cannot corroborate the story. Grey's dad is under the impression he is scared because he has done something wrong. Grey's dad gives him a lecture on the spot about why he wants to hurt me in such a manner.

Grey can only listen because his body still has not recovered from Hamp's punch. His dad apologizes on behalf of his son and they both pull off in his truck. I wish I can say this was the last altercation between us, but unfortunately, we fight a few more times before the end of the school year. Our win and loss record is about even.

After this day, Hamp and Slick always stand outside to make sure my sister and I make it home safely. They will not speak sometimes, but I eventually figure out my mother has them keep an eye on us and the house until she gets home from work. Grey eventually gives up on our feud to focus his aggression against other kids. Because I put up a good fight against Grey, most of the kids are not intimidated by him anymore. Grey and I remain friends in the neighborhood, but I keep him at a distance. As we get older, we become more civilized towards each other and talk if I see him when I go and visit the old neighborhood.

As a young third grader, I spend a lot of time by myself. This is where I begin to pick up the game of golf. This is uncommon in my area because the kids in my neighborhood are enthralled with football and basketball. Since my aunt and uncle have access to a golf course outside their backyard, I can practice a lot when I visit their house. During the fall and winter months, I spend a lot of time in the house because of daylight savings time. I still practice chip shots into a bucket in the evenings before the sun sets at five.

Sometimes, I climb a tree in our backyard and often wonder why I am not around people who look like me. I often imagine what my life would be like if I am around the European, Caucasian race, or even in a multicultural environment. I fantasize about being able to go to school and not worry about being the outcast. I imagine blending in like a chameleon. If I do get into a fight, it is over something more meaningful than the way I look. These daydreams often lead to me to wonder why my father is not here to assist me with my struggles.

I also escape reality by reading a lot of books. Most of my readings are the classics by Charles Dickens and Stephen Crane. As I get older, I immerse myself in reading the books of the *Bible*, Muhammad Ali's poetry, science fiction, comic books, and any subject detailing specific areas of history. Any work of literature helping me escape reality, I am reading it. While in my room during the fall and winter months, I wonder why I am in this world and what my purpose is in life. Seems a lot for a nine-year-old to wonder about, but I am struggling to find an identity. This is also when I start to focus on golf more and more as an escape from my current struggles. The reason I focus on the game so much is because all the golfers on television look like me. I figure I can play this game to avoid being discriminated against because of my skin complexion.

Finding an identity is almost shattered as a kid when my friend, Red—who visits his grandmother during the summer from out of state—and I are humiliated by some older kids who live on our street. Red is a lot like me, we both have single mothers and barely know our fathers. We click together when we first meet. Red does not want to go home sometimes, so he camps out at our house. Red gets a kick out of hearing his grandmother call his name to come home. His grandmother hollers his name so loud; you can literally feel her voice bouncing off the trees. Red's grandmother's house is right across the street from Slick's house. So, when Red hides out at my house, he is not too far away from home.

Red and I are playing in my front yard when some older kids on the street talk us into coming to one of their houses, which is about four homes up from mine. The kids notice how we walk to Roger's corner store often throughout the day, located about a block and a half away from my house. They observe Red drinking the same type of soda. They call us over to see if we want some extras they have left over from a picnic outing. I am skeptical at first, but Red is always hungry and thirsty.

"Hey, guys! You can get the sodas half priced compared to what you are being charged at the store." The group of older teenagers tells us.

"Half priced? Man, I will buy them." Red reacts as though this is the deal of a lifetime and gives them the money without a second thought.

Red downs the first soda with ease, but there is a catch to the second one. We both must share it. Red is not ecstatic about the deal because he paid for the sodas but eventually gives in to the demand. I am standing in the background because something does not feel right. One of the teenagers tells us he is going to get some ice and returns with two cups we must drink simultaneously. As naïve kids, Red is ready to

19

drink but I am still reluctant about sharing the soda. As we both drink, we get the biggest surprise. They urinated in the cups. Red takes off running and vomiting at the same time. I do something stupid by throwing the cup in one of the kid's faces before quickly dashing home. I enter the house and because of the charge of my entry, my mother immediately asks me what is wrong. I am embarrassed at first, but I eventually tell her what happened. She immediately charges out the door to confront all five kids. These guys can easily bum rush or knock her out, but my mom cusses and fusses even as she tells their parents what happened. I do not stick around for the outcome. I go back into the house, rinse my mouth out with antiseptic and close myself off in my room.

A few years later, a couple of the guys bring this incident up while just hanging out and talking in one of our driveways. They all apologize, except for the kid who I hit in the face with the urine. He has a look on his face like he wants to beat my brains out, but he will not gain any accolades for it. An idle mind is the devil's workshop. This trend will eventually affect a lot of the kids in my neighborhood. Being bored is the root cause leading to a lot of these guys' downfall.

This incident shatters me. I do not understand why anyone would want to do something like this to a couple of kids. Am I so low in God's eyes that he allows someone to literally treat me in the lowest way possible a human being can be treated? I really feel I am the lowest person on Earth due to the abuse at school, this incident, and my father not being around. The demons representing the sin of anger surface for the first time. The demons advise me to not lash out just yet because my time will come. I am advised to start repressing my anger internally because I may embarrass myself if I try to express it outwardly. I feel like I am not wanted in my current surroundings. These feelings cause me to become an introvert and withdrawn to strangers. I am extremely frustrated and confused. The only time I feel comfortable is on the golf course. Being on the golf course feels like my personal sanctuary. I can express myself just like Southern Baptists on Sundays. Instead of shouting and praising loudly I can express myself through my play without repercussion.

Hole 3 – Being a Boy

A few days after this incident, my sister and I are off to visit my grandparents in Virginia. I cannot wait until we board the airplane. I always feel free and secure during a flight. I love sitting back, looking out the window, and getting my thoughts together. Once we arrive, it is about a thirty-minute ride to my mother's hometown of Petersburg from the airport. I consider my grandparent's home a castle, even though it is the same size as the house we have back home. The house is in a middle-class area but is right across from the town's public housing project.

Once we settle in, I cannot wait to tell my grandparents everything I experienced during the school year. I know I bore them to death. However, they act like they are listening. What I love the most about my confessions is my grandmother telling me what I did and didn't do wrong. Her advice, as strange as I think it is sometimes, soaks in like a sponge. I love the fact someone is listening to me. It is hard to get words in with my sister around because she can talk her butt off. Even to this day, she is still talking her butt off. Regardless of the talking and snitching between my sister and me, I love her dearly. We may argue and fight like normal brothers and sisters, but we always have each other's back. In clutch circumstances, we will defend each other to the death.

My grandparent's neighbors all have grandkids about our age, so we are able to play outside during the late evening. Next door are two brothers I play with daily until they move away a few years later. These guys gave me my first introduction to baseball. It is more of a stick ball version, but it is the basic rules. We play until we are called to come inside. Both brothers are exceptional athletes who ended up playing college football at a one of the biggest programs in the state. The younger brother is arguably one of the best athletes I have ever seen. He can throw, bat, and flat out run like a gazelle. His older brother is the strong one who gets the best of his younger brother. All day, we compete to see who has the best time running the bases from short runs to first base to who has the best time running from home to home. I put up good numbers, but nothing compared to these guys. We challenge each other to hit the ball to specific spots and to see who can hit the ball the farthest. I do not win most of the competitions, but it teaches me how to work hard to win.

There are also kids whose grandparents live in a row of houses behind my grandparent's. The section of houses has open backyards, allowing everyone to cut between houses with ease. Some nights, when the adults are in someone's backyard hanging out, we have the best hide and seek games in the dark. Whoever's turn it is to be 'it', struggles for hours trying to find everyone. During one game, I find the perfect hiding spot under an apple tree in my grandmother's backyard. It reminds me of the tree I have back home. Even though I am in the middle of a game, I hide in this spot and pretend I am shutting myself off from the world. I feel like I am behind a non-translucent sheet. As the person comes by searching, I pretend I am sticking my head out of the sheet, wondering if they realize where I am. In this dark, dirty little hiding spot, I feel like I am in the most secure place imaginable. Though it is dark and filthy, I focus and see with ease. With bright clarity I wonder why I look the way I do, why am I not in a situation where I can be around others who can look over my outer shell and judge me for who I am on the inside. At an early age, I feel prejudice from those around me because I do not fit the normal racial profile. I am tired of the stares. When my grandfather takes us out to eat on the weekends, people gaze in the restaurants, especially when we address my grandparents as 'grandma' and 'grandpa.' My grandfather is passive, so he does not pay them any mind. My Grandmother is just the opposite. She blurts out a few "What the hell are you staring at?" a few times or gives a mean stare in return. Grandma is serious; she does not take mess from others. These types of situations are preparing me for a lot of stares in the future. I am thankful I am learning how to handle this at an early age.

On a pleasant day during the summer, we are over an uncle's house for a family barbeque. This uncle is my grandmother's younger brother, who is about the same age as my mother. This uncle is a trooper. He can stay out all night and still get up to make it to work on time. He has a daughter who is my age. There are many nights we stay over his house during the summer. We challenge ourselves to see if we can stay up until he makes it home. We fail miserably on several occasions. How this guy does it is a mystery. Once we get a little older, we are informed he was a supervisor with the City's Maintenance Department. He drives a truck and goes to the job site for the day, supervising the other workers while he catches up on his rest. My uncle's house is next door to my grandmother's best friend. They, too, have an open backyard connecting both houses. Her house serves as my grandmother's drinking spot, and apparently a host of others. If Bacardi knew how much of their product is consumed in this house, they probably will agree to sponsor a couple of their drinking nights.

During the barbeque, my cousin and I are challenging each other to see who can swing the highest and jump the farthest off the swing. We have challenged each other on numerous occasions, but this one is the most intense. My sister is in the background taking advantage of me trailing behind. On the last jump, I am swinging high. I mean, high enough where the swing feels as though it is coming off the foundation. As I am about to jump, I feel an extra push, which throws my timing off as I reach the top of the swing, causing me to release at the wrong time. While I am flying in the air for a few moments before hitting the ground, I know I am in trouble. In those milliseconds, I am trying to force my body to land somewhat safely. I am trying to figure out a fall that will cause the least amount of pain. My cousin is in such awe of my flight, she ignores the brick flowerbed border and trips into a cactus.

While coming in for an emergency landing, I decide I will try to land feet first and then roll to ease the inevitable pain I am about to feel. As I land, I do an amazing job coming in feet first. However, I misjudge my body's momentum. I hit the ground and bounce immediately off my feet into a forward tumble.

During the tumbling, I hear a '*snap*' and a sting in my hand as I try to break my momentum. During my emergency landing, I manage to break my wrist and piss off a bumblebee enough during my roll for it to sting me.

After releasing out a huge cry, my grandmother rushes over to see if I am okay as the other adults are trying to get the cactus needles out of my cousin's behind. My wrist does not hurt, but the bee sting is causing excruciating pain. My grandmother concocts an old, home pain remedy for the bee sting by cutting open a cigarette, wetting the tobacco with hot sauce (where the hot sauce appears from during the chaos is a mystery), and applying it to my sting. In an instant, the swelling, the bee's stinger, and the pain go away.

While riding to the ER, I am so dumbfounded by the disappearance of the bee sting, I totally forget about my wrist. Until they take me back in the ER and hold my thumb up in a netting to analyze my wrist. I guess my grandmother still has her mother's intuition, because she comes back to the room without being called by a nurse.

"Ma'am, you will have to leave. Only parents or guardians are allowed." The nurse states to my grandmother, due to the perception she is looking for a black patient.

"I am here for my grandson." My grandmother replies as I reach out to her.

The nurses and ER doctor are quite stunned. They pause for a few moments, wondering how in the hell this Caucasian-looking child is related to this dark-skinned woman. I see the look in their eyes that I must have been adopted or kidnapped. Before they begin mending my wrist, they get my mother on the phone to see if I am allergic to any medicines. I see the nurse turn her head away from the table while she is on the phone with my mother. I wonder if she is asking my mom to describe my grandmother to make sure nothing criminal is occurring. As I look back on this incident, I can imagine my grandmother getting wind of the nurse's conversation with my mother. I believe she would have torn up the county hospital.

Once the nurses and doctors get over the shock and start mending me back together, I start to tell them how my grandmother swooped in after I fell and quickly started first aid on my sting. I describe the tobacco and hot sauce remedy. The room suddenly gets quiet again.

"My grandmother did something similar on mosquito bites." The ER doctor states to break the silence.

"Yeah! We did not have a choice when I was young. We could not afford a doctor for minor things." my grandmother replies.

My grandmother is a little tipsy because she starts going on and on about little things you can do at home for minor first aid treatments. The more the hospital staff asks questions or share similar stories; the more my grandmother gives them scenarios and recipes. The most amusing remedies to everyone are the ones involving corn whiskey. She is right about the corn whiskey. Good corn whiskey will remove all impurities from your body.

During the ride home from the hospital, I replay the day's events in my head. I am convinced my sister deliberately pushed me out of the swing. It was probably payback for something I did to her, and she felt this was the perfect time for revenge. My sister and I have the typical brother and sister relationship. We do things to each other to retaliate for snitching to my mother or when one of us will not cooperate with one another.

"Homer, what happened this afternoon? Surely you did not think you could fly?" my mother asks via a long-distance phone call.

"In a sense, I was trying to fly for a moment." I reply.

My grandfather intervenes to soothe my mother's nerves by convincing her the incident is due to a boy just being a boy.

Hole 4 – Coming of Age

Once summer winds$ down, we are back in our hometown. We normally return the week or weekend before school starts. I question why a mother would allow her kids to stay away from home for so long. As an adult with three kids, my mother sending us off to visit our grandparents is a brilliant idea. We need to spend time with her side of the family to have a relationship with her kin. Because we are living in my father's hometown, we already have established relationships with his relatives. My mother probably saved a fortune on not having to worry about childcare, gas, and the hustle parents go through shuttling kids back and forth. Most importantly, she uses the time with us being away to get herself centered and her nerves back in order. My mother is raising two close age kids by herself while trying to maintain a career. I promised myself whenever I got married, I would never let my wife experience this type of hardship. My wife and I struggle to raise the ones we have together, but I can't imagine if either one of us had to do it by ourselves. We both have good careers and put a lot of effort into our crafts. However, it takes a lot of energy to keep up with our kids. We love them dearly, but we always look forward to having some time away with only the two of us.

My fourth and fifth grade years are typical. The years go by without any major incidents at school. I have some good teachers and remain an honor roll student. I have some altercations here and there but nothing on the scale of what Grey and I went through the years before. My uncle enters me into some junior golf tournaments to assess my skill set. These tournaments are quite amusing. I am the only minority participating in these events and the white kids can tell I am not one of them but they cannot figure out my ethnic background. Instead of coming out and asking, I am ostracized during the events. Some kids barely shake my hand after a match or round of golf. When we break for lunch or rest between matches, I normally eat a sandwich under a huge shade tree while talking with my uncle or aunt, reviewing my play.

During a training session where we are paired in groups of four, I try to join my group during a break under a tree just to converse until our instructor returns. As soon as I sit under the tree, these guys move to another tree. This is when I begin to wonder if my appearance is truly a curse. I learn to adapt to the kids at school treating me this way, but these are kids who look like me and I am still being rejected. While sitting under a tree waiting to begin playing, I grasp the reality I am an outcast. It is funny how God works because he gives me a remedy to handle these circumstances. He has given me the gift of understanding the game of golf. He blesses me with the ability and passion to want to play. Once I gain passion for the game, I start playing at a high level. I win my fair share of junior tournaments and play well enough to be in contention in all my events. When I am shunned by kids at an event or camp, I start to disregard them because I now have the confidence and ability to play them competitively on the golf course. I know I can beat them like they stole something at any given time. Due to my play, I eventually begin to gain these guys' respect and they start to accept me once they get to know me.

My life changes when my mother and grandfather put up a basketball net in our backyard. I learn to practice on my own and develop a textbook jump shot. Red normally sneaks into the backyard to practice when he thinks no one is home. He ignores the neighbors request to leave when they can't see me in the backyard with him. Red normally wins in one-on-one games. However, I kill him in skill games like 'horse', 'punk', or whatever derogatory name we can come up with to describe the loser.

By this time, Red is living full time with his grandmother. I am not sure of the reason, but I think it is because Red's mother is struggling as a single parent. She is not as fortunate to have the same support group as my mother. In the back of Red's mind, I think he is under the impression his mother has given up on him. Red is set back a grade due to an issue with his transcripts from out of state. Due to all these issues, Red becomes rebellious and gives whoever has authority a hard time. His only solace is playing basketball.

Gangs begin moving into our neighborhood from the Chicago area. At first, they are not recruiting kids our age. They target the middle school kids and only let those join who come to them for initiation. The genre of hip-hop and gangster rap music is also beginning to surface in our lives. I am fortunate to like all genres of music. MTV plays a huge role in the music I listen to and enjoy. I fall in love with the 'hair bands' because of the guitar solos. I like rap music, also. I tune into MTV after school to watch the top five rock videos to piss Red off. The combination of street life and the hip-hop culture intrigues Red. Red gives me a hard time about taking my schoolwork and golf so seriously. I really do not have a choice. My mother will literally raise all kind of hell if we bring anything lower than a 'B' home on our report cards.

If I do not keep my grades up, I cannot play golf or baseball, period. No negotiating!

After school, Red goes everywhere but home. My routine is to go home and knock out whatever homework I have so I can go outside as soon as my mother gets home from work. Before doing anything, I must show my mother my completed assignments, especially before going to a golf coaching session or baseball practice. If Red cannot find anywhere to hang out, he often yells below my bedroom window to challenge me to a one-on-one basketball contest. If I am busy, I often let him go around back and I join him when I am finished.

This is also the time when home video games become popular. If it is raining or cold out, Red hides out from his grandmother in my room, playing Nintendo or Atari. He tries to coerce me from doing homework by challenging me to a game. Both Red and I are highly competitive, but I know my schoolwork is more important. Red gets frustrated with me if I challenge him to try to do his assignments. Red can do the work, he is smart and quite sharp. In my opinion, he is purposely holding himself back to try to gain his mother's attention. Red figures if his mother knew how bad he is struggling adapting to life without seeing her daily, she will come and take him back to live with her. This eventually happens. Unfortunately, by the time she comes back a few years later, Red is a lost cause.

Slick and Hamp still make sure my sister and I arrive home safely every day. Slick often strikes up a conversation just to see how things are going since I am getting older. Slick knows I am infatuated with airplanes and aerodynamics. He makes remote control airplanes and lets Red and I watch him fly them around the neighborhood. Slick eventually earns my mother's trust to look after me after school, help me out with some of the advanced classes I am taking in school, taking me to practices, and to go with him when he runs errands for his parents. Slick even babysits sometimes when my mother goes out on Friday nights. Normally, we go over to my paternal grandmother's house, but I think my mother thinks my grandma is beginning to slow down a bit. My preference is to go over my aunt's house, but they are still hitting the streets themselves.

Slick has a friend, Briggs, who lives in the cove at the end of our street with his grandmother. Briggs is an ex-military guy who has experience in the Marines, which makes you think he is sort of crazy. Briggs takes his monthly military check and asks Slick to drop him off at the strip club on the first Friday of every month. He always tells Slick he will call him when he is ready to come home. I don't know what time this usually is, but I know it is after my mom gets home and I am sound asleep. Briggs serves as the neighborhood quarterback for football games on the schoolyard. This dude should have played college football somewhere because his arm is like a cannon.

The games normally pit the two apartment complexes close to our school against each other. These guys are some hard dudes. They are the ones the gangs have targeted. They take to the lifestyle with full force. These guys do not care about anything. They use the football games as a source of stress relief from everyday street life and the complications of growing up poor without much hope of making it out of their circumstances. The apartment complexes are affiliated with the same gang, but they are sworn enemies when it comes to the football and basketball games. Anyone can play and you do not have to necessarily live in the apartment complexes to be part of the game.

Here's how the teams are formulated; If you live on the north side of the Alcy road, which is the street dividing our neighborhood, you play for the blue apartments; If you lived on the south side of the street, you play for the White apartments. There are no rules. You get more respect staying in the field of play rather than trying to get out of bounds. You can run out of bounds if you like, but you pay dearly. You will literally get tackled on the concrete pathway leading to the front of the school or you will get lit up on the teacher's parking lot.

During one game, the blue team was short a player.

"Red, we need you to play." Briggs states.

"No way, man, I am not having any part of this." Red replies.

"Homer, come on and play. We really need you to make the numbers even." Briggs asks me.

The competitive part of me quickly jumps at the chance to play.

"Sure, why not!" I reply.

The truth is, I am afraid of the consequences if I turn the invitation down. If I do not play, these guys will classify me as weak or soft. They already have the preconceived notion that I am weak due to being the white kid. The captain of the blue team, Brute, pulls me to the side and explains the rules.

"These guys will not show you any mercy because you are the youngest one on the field. They will deliberately take shots at you just to feel as though they can get over on a white person. Here are a few pointers to breaking tackles, the best way to plow through blocks, and how to hit back at these guys. Regardless of how hard you get hit, do not let these guys think they have hurt you. Whatever you do, make sure you stay inbounds." Brute states as he gives me a pat on the back, which feels more like a punch.

I am fortunate most of the guys on my team remember me from the incident with Grey in the restroom a few years ago.

We start out on defense. The guy they assign me to is also the smallest one on their team. To me, being in the fifth grade, this guy looks like he is ready to get drafted by the NFL. However, I notice a look of fear in his eyes. The fear is not because of me, but of what can happen if he catches or must run the ball. As Briggs calls out, "Hike!" the field sounds like a herd of buffalo running from lions in the jungle. There are a few grunts and some yelling regarding what is about to happen. As Briggs releases the ball for a pass, I leave the man I am covering to follow the ball. While running to attempt to make a play, one of the opposing players hits me with a block, causing me to see a flash of light. I also cannot feel my body for a few seconds.

"Get up! Remember, don't let these guys think they hurt you!" Brute whispers as he attempts to pick me up from the ground.

After what feels like a few hours, I jump up after a few seconds to get back to the huddle and do it all over again.

"Hike!" Briggs calls to start the next play.

I know the ball is coming my way because the other team knows I am shaken up a bit. The competitive part of me takes over.

"I have to do this; don't give in to these guys." I say to myself repeatedly.

As predicted, the ball is in the air coming towards the guy I am defending. It is a short crossing route, and my opponent gets a good step on me. Because I am afraid of messing up two plays in a row, I try hard to stay with him stride for stride, but he is too fast. As he attempts to catch the ball, I lunge into his legs with a sweeping motion of my arms to make sure he cannot run after the catch. He is not expecting this as he turns up field. I take his legs from him, causing the ball to fly out of his hands into my teammates arms who returns it for a touchdown. I am not aware of what I have done because I hit the ground hard again. Once the play is over, these guys are lifting me up as if we have won the Super Bowl. This infuriates the other team because the rules of the game are always to win by two touchdowns, and we are already up one. If we stop them on the next possession and score, the game is over.

As the game goes on, I am literally abused from play to play. I am knocked around, stepped on, kicked, punched, scratched, and even bitten when I try to recover a fumble. On one play, I catch a pass and am immediately clotheslined by the defender. Even though I am dazed, I keep hearing Brute's voice in my head.

"Don't let these guys think they hurt you!"

No matter what these guys do to me, I jump back up, keep playing, and stay in the field of play. I need to prove I belong and receive acceptance from these guys. One guy isn't so lucky. He twists his ankle trying to cut up field with the ball and immediately goes out of bounds. Big mistake! Our team viciously tackles him on the concrete. He broke the rules and because of the street code, he is punished for it. The guy who tackles him hurts himself by skinning up his arm on the pavement. When the guy cannot continue because of his ankle, the game is over. I will admit, I am delighted.

As the guys are giving the other team a hard time for having to forfeit, Brute pulls me to the side to let me know my teammates are proud of me.

"You've got a lot of heart and it showed it on the field." One of my teammates express.

"I remembered when he first started kindergarten." Brute directs to the group.

"Yeah, he is one tough white boy." One of the guys who physically abused me during the game expresses to Brute.

Once again, they are looking at my physical appearance. They have no idea about my true ethnic background.

Brute is not a big guy, but he is muscular. A lot of the guys follow him because he is a natural leader. This guy can easily become a congressman or even mayor of Memphis if he applies himself.

Unfortunately, Brute already knows he will not fulfill any of his life's dreams by being a legitimate citizen.

"Homer. Remember, if I am around, no one will mess with you. Do me a favor and stay focused on your schoolwork. Please don't follow the example of these guys. You can penetrate the system and unlock doors for all of us.;" Brute states keenly.

As an eleven-year-old kid, I do not have a clue as to what the hell he is talking about.

Red overhears Brute giving me accolades in front of the gang. I can tell he is not happy about it.

"I should have gone with my first instinct and played. You are now in with them. Boy are you lucky." Red expresses while we walk from the schoolyard.

"It was stupid of me to play."

"Then why did you do it?"

"Because I was afraid of what may happen if I didn't play. I need to start having people judge me for my character instead of judging me because they think I am white. It would have been a long tough road to get these guys to embrace me if I showed fear and did not play."

Red keeps going on and on, talking about what to do now since I am in their inner circle. I am not paying attention to him because I am still trying to make sense of what Brute told me. All I want to do is get in a hot bathtub. Briggs catches up with us after bumming a cigarette off someone.

"Homer, you did the right thing because those guys would have classified you as weak." Briggs expresses to me before addressing Red. "Red, you will have to prove yourself to those guys at some point." Briggs statement to Red is ill advised. In my opinion, this comment starts Red down a dark pathway. Briggs is not aware of Red's infatuation with the street life and the advice given to him only fuels his desire to belong to this type of crowd.

Briggs veers off to Slick's house and Red says he will come by my house after he takes a bath. Once I get in the house, my aunt and uncle are visiting, so I go downstairs to say hello. My mother looks at me and inquiries about my appearance because I look as though I have been through a war. I am thankful my uncle is here as I explain the events of the football game. He eases the concerns from my aunt and mother. He shares with them a similar story when he was growing up and stories about their own boys having to prove themselves to others. As I go to take a bath, I hear my aunt say the kids are probably picking on me because they think I am white. Actuality, my decision to play is to *avoid* them picking on me for this reason.

After I peel off my clothes, I am looking at the scratches, the small abrasions, and the bite mark. I notice my lower face and neck are red because of the clothesline I received. I also observe some purple spots on my body I know will eventually turn into bruises. As I sit in the bathtub, I am in immense pain and the hot water is only making it worse. The longer I soak, the more the pain goes away. I am rubbing my muscles with some type of muscle cream I find in the medicine cabinet. What I do not realize is how it turns hot once it interacts with water. After about thirty minutes, I get out and immediately put on some night clothes. It is only about 7 PM, but I am exhausted. When I get to my room, Red is on the floor playing video games. I am replaying the events of the day in my head. I feel some sort of liberation for proving myself, but my body is mad as hell from the punishment. I begin to wonder what my father would think if I told him what I did today. Would he be proud? Would he give me a pat on the back as encouragement? Would he get upset? My father not being around really is messing with my internal search for an identity. I figure he can give me some type of advice. Although I feel proud of myself, I want him to be proud of me also. I wonder if I should act like Red in hopes of my father coming to pick me up and going to live with him. I quickly toss this fantasy away because I know it is unrealistic.

Once again, my demons' surface to give me some advice.

"You do not need him. If he wanted you, he would be here right now. You need to forget about him." The demons whisper in my head.

After the demons disappear, I make a vow to myself once I have children, I will let them know how much I love them and how proud I am of them whenever they do something that feels like an accomplishment. The last thing I want is for anyone to feel the way I do. Along with trying to find my identity, I feel as though a void is missing in my life and I want to fill it immediately. A commercial advertising golf balls comes on television while Red is switching out cartridges for the video game system. After the commercial is over, I decide to ride the game of golf as far as I can as I stare at a few trophies. I become conscious of the circumstances of the society I am living in at a young age. I notice the trend for the young men in our neighborhood is going toward the negative.

All these guys have the same opportunity to escape these circumstances by putting forth just a little effort in school. Most of these guys will end up in prison or dead. I cannot take this road. I do not want my dreams and goals deferred due to my surroundings. Red is talking about something as I lay across my bed. I am so tired his words are like the adult voices from the Charlie Brown cartoons. Whatever he is muttering is irrelevant to me as I drift off into a deep sleep.

Hole 5 – Adolescence

My aunt is a secretary at an elementary school in another part of the city. She thinks it will be good for me to go on a field trip with her school's sixth grade gifted class to visit a well-known cave located about two hundred miles from Memphis. I do not mind because it gives me an excuse to get away from the normal everyday routine in my neighborhood. Golf and baseball season have not started so I will not miss anything. If my aunt suggests the trip, it must be a good idea. She is one of the few people who knows my interests. Plus, I do not mind meeting kids who have the same type of curiosity as me.

At first, I am a little suspect, because once again no one on the bus looks like me. I stay close to my aunt, but I do not give her the feeling I am uncomfortable. A few of the girls on the trip walk up to my aunt inquiring about me. General questions regarding who I am in relation to her and where do I go to school. One of the girls asks me if I want to join them where they are sitting. When I sit down, I make eye contact with a girl. She isn't bad looking. She has light brown skin, wavy hair, and she's wearing a perfect pair of glasses. We strike up a quick conversation, introducing ourselves to each other. Her name is Ally. The guys in the group are playing cards and trying to keep it away from the chaperones on the trip. I notice these guys are amateurs to the card game but are talking it up as adults do to try and impress the folks watching them play. I know this game very well because my older cousins taught me how to play at a young age. I am whispering to Ally, telling her all the moves the players are about to execute.

Another girl overhears me whispering and states I must know how to play very well. She says it loud enough for the guys playing to hear. Ally suggests they let me play. Of course, the first thing from one of the players is, "This white boy can't play our card game." Once again, my competitive side and the need to prove I belong takes over and I do not hesitate to join in the game. Plus, my demons surface again to tell me to try to disgrace them in front of their peers. My cousins taught me how to look at the way the dealer shuffles the cards, how the cards are cut, and watch how the cards are dealt. To everyone's surprise, I immediately call out the dealer when I see he is pulling from the bottom of the deck. My playing partner's eyes light up with excitement because he knows the odds of winning have dramatically increased after unmasking their tactics.

When the game starts, I notice our opponents are giving signals to let each other know what to play. I immediately advise my playing partner about our opponents' tactics and tell him not to worry.

"We will win easily because these guys are rookies." I advise my playing partner, which gets a rise out of those spectating.

Just as I predict, we win the game easily. Our foes are so surprised they are losing, they do not notice me using the same card twice to cheat them out of a score. We are playing a rise and fly format so everyone can play. After we beat the first set of guys, I play honestly. I want to beat those guys because of the statement they made about my appearance. Statements like this are one of the reasons I am struggling to find an identity. I am tired of feeling I must prove myself and show

I do fit in with my own people. I played for about forty-five more minutes until I lose on purpose. Ally never leaves my side. I forfeit the game because I want to talk to her and get to know her a little better.

My playing partner tells me Ally is the prettiest girl in the class and she rejects all guys' advances at their school. Once again, my competitive side takes over. Currently in our lives, we are happy to get a girl to tell us if they like us or not. We are not interested in getting their phone numbers yet. As I start a conversation, we both have similar interests. We both like Prince over Michael Jackson, our birthdays are six days apart, and we both like MTV. Liking MTV stunned me, I never thought this girl would go for the genre of music played on MTV. We talk about the bands, the songs, the VJ's, and our favorite show, *Friday Night Video Fights*. We both disagree on the last show when Def Leppard's 'Photograph' beat out Van Halen's 'Jump.' Ally gives her reasons Van Halen should have won, and I give my reasons why Def Leppard won. We discuss Whitney Houston and how I feel she is a one album wonder. I debate she will never reach the heights of Gladys Knight. Boy was I wrong.

We finish our conversation because we have arrived at our destination. Still feeling a little uncomfortable, I immediately link up with my aunt once we get off the bus. To my surprise, the guys I beat playing cards and my playing partner quickly ask if I want to be part of their group. An even bigger surprise is Ally and her friends also wanting to be part of our group. Without hesitation, I join them.

The actual tour of the cave is very interesting. There are some tight spots we navigate through. I have a lot of questions and I think I get on the tour guide's nerves with some of my inquiries. Some of the terrain is slippery and at points where Ally thinks she will fall, she grabs my hand. When Ally first grabs my hand, it feels a little weird. The only girl's hand I ever held was my sister's and I did not get this feeling from her holding my hand. Me being curious, I quickly want to feel this sensation again. I want to make sure I am not imagining what I just felt. When she grabs my hand a second time, I hold on a little while longer to see if Ally and I were both having the same feeling. Apparently, we are on the same page. When this happens again, Ally holds on a little longer and blushes when our eyes lock.

During the sixth grade, I am developing physically. I am tall for my age and skinny as a rail, but the green eyes, my skin complexion, and hair always lure the girls to want to touch it. In the past, it was always the older girls, and I think they are just teasing, which made me think something is wrong my appearance. In this instance, this is a girl my age and we are both mutually attracted to each other.

We eat at a buffet-style restaurant before heading back home. I notice Ally looking at me while I am eating. We are at different tables because I decide to eat with my aunt. My aunt draws my attention away from Ally for a moment to tell me she can tell I am having a good time. I was afraid she noticed my attraction to Ally, but she tells me it is because I am smiling and conversing freely with others. I thank her for letting me come on the trip. I feel as though the reason I am open and carefree right now is because of the group noticing who I am and not looking at my outer appearance. It also helps to break out of your shell when a pretty girl has your attention.

While boarding the bus, Ally whispers if I want to sit next to her on the long ride home. I nod my head in agreement. We talk more as the sun sets and it gets dark on the bus. When it is completely dark, Ally grabs my hand, and we enjoy each other's conversation on the ride back to Memphis. The chaperones start walking through the bus to advise us we were about twenty miles out, Ally totally shocks me once the chaperone heads to the front of the bus with her back to us. She reaches over, turns my head to hers, and kisses me. My eyes pop open and I jerk a bit when she attempts to slip her tongue in my mouth, but Ally tells me to relax. I am more concerned with getting caught, but she has her group of friends shielding the view in a way so what we are doing doesn't look suspicious.

The feeling from kissing her is amazing. I have been kissed by relatives on the cheek and this doesn't feel like the kisses from my grandmother on the forehead. The kissing is igniting some feelings I have never felt before from a girl. I am like a flower waking up in the spring. I just had my first real kiss and my attitude toward life has changed.

Once we arrive back at the school, Ally is rushed from the scene because her mother is in a hurry. We do not exchange phone numbers or any type of contact information. I never see her again, but I want to thank her for giving me the feelings I found during the trip. When I leave with my aunt, I feel as though I have a new beginning and I'm about to move forward to a new stage in my life. I just entered the world of puberty. The guys on the trip told me Ally was a challenge and I feel like I have conquered a difficult task. My confidence soars.

When I return to school after this trip, I feel new and revived. I am curious about what my body is going through, but researching these topics is not easy. I really do not know who to turn to or ask, so I kind of shelve my questions. Apparently, the other guys' testosterone in my class are starting to surface. Before my first kiss, I never notice how the girls in my class are much more developed compared to the boys. After kissing Ally, I begin paying attention to the girls in much more detail. Some of the guys sit around at recess and talk about how they have already lost their virginity. I know they are lying, but the creativity behind their stories is entertaining. Reading between the lines, these guys have an experience like I do and think this feeling means they have progressed into manhood.

Grey is the biggest storyteller. His tales seem to come strictly from a *Playboy* magazine. According to Grey, he starts having sex at eight years old. One afternoon during recess, some of the guys question his stories in disbelief, causing Grey to become enraged. Grey's come back is always to compare penis sizes. Grey's theory is your penis fully develops once you start having sex. Of course, these guys have enough sense not to give into Grey's unproven scientific hypothesis. Grey gets extremely frustrated because we are not buying into his story. His irritation causes him to stand up, pull his pants down, and expose himself to the guys in the group. This is a huge mistake. The guys start heckling him about doing this in front of other boys and this is when the gay rumors start to swirl. Once the story gets back to the girls in the group, Grey will try to use this as a pickup line to get a girl to like him.

Unfortunately, the girls feel only a gay man will expose themselves to a bunch of guys. Grey's attempt to prove the rumors are false will haunt him through to the end of our sixth-grade year.

My grades are top notch and I score high on our state standardized tests. According to my test results, my learning capacity is on an eleventh-grade level, and I am in the top five percent in my class. Our school is going through an overhaul. The students in the top five percentile are tasked with starting up the computer and science labs. I accept the task of the computer lab because most of my classmates are intimidated by the new technology. Most of them feel the science lab will be an easier challenge. Once again, my competitive side wants the difficult task in order to prove something to myself.

My principal is the overseer of the computer lab because this is where most of the money will be donated and spent.

Three students will go with our principal to different events during school hours to present our cause to businesses in the community in hopes of raising money. I do not mind the field trips because we normally get a nice free lunch after the presentations. My principal tells my sixth-grade teacher to allow me to go with her to visit the corporation who adopted our school in a last-ditch effort to raise money for our computer lab. I tell my teacher I really do not want to go, but the principal insists.

"Showing the corporation we have white children in our school will help our cause tremendously." I overhear her telling my teacher.

My principal's strategy works because we get more than enough money from the company to get top of the line equipment for the science lab also. In the mid-80s, 99% of corporate America is white. School funding is tight, forcing my principal to use every advantage she has to finance this project. At first, I am upset I am used in such a manner. In the end, I think it is a brilliant move by my principal. I finally understand what Brute was trying to convey to me. I can use my appearance to blend into an environment and use my knowledge of the system to benefit myself and others.

After getting the money, my principal lets us pick out the computers and the learning software we will use to get the lab up and running. This is my first true hard work experience. At first, there are three of us, but one of the students in my group comes down with a case of the chicken pox and is out of school for six weeks. It is up to me, and a girl named Free to get everything running by the deadline my principal sets. To get the full donation, we must show our sponsor we are serious about this venture. Free and I spend a lot of time alone in the room housing the lab. We spend about two hours in class to get our general instruction and then work in the computer lab the rest of the day. Free is extremely developed for her age and she knows it. Free was held back from starting kindergarten a year because her birthday falls outside of the state mandated window for kids to start attending school. I am eleven going on twelve and she is twelve going on thirteen. I notice a lot of older guys in our neighborhood trying to flirt with her during my walks to Roger's corner store. She teases the guys the best she can to get them to buy her goods from the store. I understand how she attracts male attention due to her curvaceous figure. Free is built like a freshman in high school more so than a girl in the sixth grade. The only issue is Free has the mentality of a child in the sixth grade. I never notice how developed Free is until we start spending a lot of time alone. Unknowingly to Free, I often stare at her body, daydreaming while she is setting up paper in a printer or bending over to setup a cable in the back of a computer. Once again, I start to feel things in my body. I am trying to figure out the sensation coming over me.

After the technicians get all the hardware setup, Free and I start to get familiar with the software we picked out with our principal. We quickly master the Print Shop and Word Processing software on the system. Our principal is amazed at the banners, signs, and newsletters we develop and distribute. She uses our work to show our sponsor why the lab is so important. She instructs every teacher to send their newsletters home to parents for us to design and print. The principal also wants us to print all banners and signs going on the teacher's bulletin boards. Our work will show our sponsor the benefits of having a lab in-house and how it can be utilized all over the school. This means Free and I will spend a lot of time together getting these projects completed.

One day after school, Free startles me by stating she notices how look at her.

"What do you mean?" I ask, denying her observation.

"It is okay because a lot of guys look at me this way. Frankly, I love the attention."

As a kid beginning puberty, I am intrigued as to where this is leading. While I am standing by a printer waiting for it to finish a banner, Free comes behind me and starts rubbing her hands through my hair. The strokes with her hand feel so good I almost fall asleep. The baffling sensation quickly surfaces.

"I have had a crush on you since the third grade Homer." Free whispers as my spine tingles from her touch.

The sensation is causing me not to have the ability to respond to her confessions.

"Homer, are you a virgin?"

"Yes!" I reply without hesitation.

Free then starts to kiss my cheek until I turn her head towards mine and begin to kiss her like Ally kissed me.

"Where did you learn a move like that?" Free asks while beginning to laugh.

"This is not my first kiss."

The computer lab is located on the top floor of our school at the far end of the hall. We do not have to worry about someone walking in on us because we can hear footsteps approaching from the hollow hallway that magnifies any sound.

As Free kisses me, I quickly get distressed because I begin to feel uncomfortable in a certain area. In haste, I pull back from Free, gather my things and take off towards home. My pace is swift as I run into Red. I mistakenly tell Red what just happened with Free. Red starts going on and on about what he would have done in this type of situation. He refers to the different positions he will put her in and how he will make her holler out his name. At first, I am wondering how Red knows about positions, but I am afraid to find out where he has conducted his research. Red's uncles live with his grandmother, and he discovers their porn magazines and videos. I quickly excuse myself from Red by telling him I have a lot of homework to complete. I feel embarrassed because I am not sure what to do in this type of situation.

No one has talked to me about sex. I know you cannot raise your hand and ask the teacher about sex as a question in class. I know I cannot walk up to my mother and tell her what I am feeling. I can see my mother losing her mind. I really want to reach out to my father, but I am afraid of his reaction. Plus, I am not sure if he will take my phone call.

Once I am home, all I can think about is Free. I must do something to get my mind off what just happened. I decide to go out back and practice chipping golf balls into a bucket I place around the yard to master accuracy. This does not take my mind off Free, so I play basketball for a little while. Once I start dribbling, I know it is only a short amount of time before Red joins me. To my surprise, Grey accompanies Red into the backyard.

"Did you mention to Grey about what happen between Free and I? I don't want Grey to know anything about my interaction with Free." I ask Red in a whisper.

"No, Grey just pulled around on his bike right as I was walking up the driveway. I know he has a crush on her. I have heard his lies about having sex with her."

I feel a sigh of relief because the last thing I need is an altercation with Grey right now.

We quickly start up a game of twenty-one and for some reason, my game is astonishing. I am frustrating Red because my jumpers are falling from all over the court. Grey is no contest because I can dribble by him with ease. When they both try to double team me, I split between the both for easy layups. After winning three or four games in a row, Red begs me to play him one-on-one. We are about to start when suddenly, we hear a rumble in the dense trees aligning the back fence of my house. This massive kid appears from the trees asking if he can join us. His introduces himself as Telly. Red and I give our greetings. You can tell by the greeting between Grey and Telly they will never like each other.

Telly's folks just rented a house behind ours. You can tell by Telly's clothes and shoes his family is struggling financially. Telly is a year older than us and will enroll at the local middle school in our area. I really do not care about his financial struggles or background. I want to see if he can play ball or not. We end up playing two-on-two with Red and Grey facing off against Telly and me. I am so focused on getting my mind off Free, Telly and I end up winning four out of five games. Telly and Greys' physical play leads to an immediate rivalry between the two. Red is completely frustrated by losing. Red never wants to lose against me in anything. However, when you are in the zone, there is no defense to contain it. After going in the house for the evening, I feel good after my performance on the court.

The next day at school, I cannot wait to see Free. Once we are alone, I quickly explain the events yesterday had nothing to do with her. I talk for an hour about the way my body was feeling and the sensation I discovered.

"If you feel uncomfortable, I will back off." Free responds to my babbling.

Even though this is what I am hoping will happen, my hormones telling my body something different.

"What is your relationship with Grey?" I ask Free before we begin any type of physical interaction.

"Grey follows me around like a lovesick puppy and he shows up on my doorstep begging me to be his girlfriend." Free states while laughing.

"Did you have sex with Grey?"

"Hell, no, Homer! My only sexual encounter was with one of my brother's friends. It hurt so bad it will be a while before I do something like that again. I do like kissing and touching." Free states while chuckling some more.

Now in the back of my mind, I am stuck on Free emphasizing the pain she felt. The feeling I had yesterday was painful as well. Pain stays in my head for a long time when I come close to having a physical encounter like this one I experienced with Free.

"I do like you, Homer. Do you want to be my boyfriend?"

"I guess so. I never had a girlfriend before."

"Good. It is nice to know I am the first."

"We must keep this a secret. I am not up to any confrontations with Grey." I emphasize to Free.

"That's fine with me." Free states as we begin to kiss again.

Free is my first girlfriend, but a great distance from being my first love.

It is easy keeping our relationship a secret because we have different sixth grade teachers. We kiss a few more times and hold hands on the way home, cutting through the wooded area separating the school from our neighborhood. Her aunt lives at the top of my street, so it is not a problem going in the same direction. Once the computer lab is complete, our time together quickly dwindles, causing us to mutually call off the relationship. The breakup does not affect me, and we share one last kiss. After meeting Ally, having successfully started up the computer lab, and the relationship with Free, I am feeling pretty good about myself. I am walking with a positive mindset and looking forward to whatever new adventures come my way.

Hole 6 – Chaos

I compete in a few more schoolyard football games during my sixth-grade year. The games are becoming too fierce. The gang presence is becoming more abundant. Players are showing up to the games armed, high, and angry at the world. Red joins in the games and quickly becomes a force to reckon with on the field. He can catch anything thrown his way. I am making a name for myself on the defensive side of the ball due to hard hits I put on the opposing players. Some of these hits lead to some physical altercations but Brute always intervenes before things get out of hand. Brute removes himself from the games and gets a thrill from being a spectator. Brute is now heavily involved with dealing drugs. He shows up to the games with his Rottweiler dogs, brand new sneakers, and his huge radio. Brute is my biggest supporter; he puts money on us to win and places side bets with new spectators to show his confidence in my ability to shut down the other team's best receiver. Most of the guys think it is a sucker bet due to my appearance. I do not look a dominant player. However, I am pure hell when the ball is snapped.

Red's cousin, Dirty, begins to visit more frequently and participates in the games whenever we have one when he is in the neighborhood. Dirty is our age but is a physical specimen to be twelve years old. We accidentally collide once while making a tackle on an opposing player. It was like hitting a stone wall. Dirty lives in the Whitehaven area of Memphis and goes to a different school. When the guys at the game first meet him, they quickly want to challenge him to see if Dirty has the pedigree to play in our games. They give Dirty the same treatment they gave me at first. Conversely, one play quickly ceases the challenging.

Dirty is never made aware of the out of bounds rule and runs to the sideline on the first pass he catches. The opposing team quickly lays into him with some fierce tackles on the pavement. Dirty is not stunned by the hits.

"Give me the fucking ball again." Dirty instructs Briggs while we are huddling to call the next play.

"Hike!" Briggs yells out once we are set on the line of scrimmage.

Dirty grabs the ball from Briggs and takes off up field, flirting with the sideline. To the opposing team's amazement, Dirty deliberately steps out of bounds to end the play. Everyone not close to the sideline immediately stops their forward progression in disbelief to what they are witnessing. Everyone pauses to see the carnage about to occur.

In what looks like a scene from a movie, Dirty stiff arms one guy straight to the concrete. As the second guy approaches, he shoulder blocks the guy straight to the pavement and gives a vicious elbow to the third guy. All three of these guys hit the concrete with a huge, '*thud*'!

"Now, try that shit again." Dirty hollers out to everyone on the opposing team. As the gang's members start to circle around Dirty, Brute intervenes.

"Remember, there are no rules. You guys must learn how to accept the punishment you dish out." Brute reiterates to the group.

Red and I do not know what to expect after this incident. Once the game resumes, there is a target on Dirty's back. Dirty does not mind because he gets a thrill from the challenge. The game is easy after this incident because the opposing team is not sure know how to handle Dirty. We win the game, but the battles are far from over.

After the game, Red congregates with the gang members. If Brute wins a significant amount of money, he gives me some of his winnings for my efforts. He wants to give me more money than I will accept. However, I know my mother will be suspicious if she finds a lot of money in my room. I take enough to get some snacks from the store. Each time I see Brute, he gives me a hard time about playing golf. He is just teasing, but deep down he does not understand why I have a passion for the game.

While Red is congregating and trying to listen to the rap music on Brute's huge boom box, Dirty and I drift off to the store because we know hanging around these guys is trouble waiting to happen. Dirty is the only person who can keep Red focused and sway him out of trouble. Once we return from the store, Dirty gets in Red's face about hanging out with these guys. Red tries to rigorously argue his point to no avail. Red is afraid of Dirty and knows how far he can push his luck with him without repercussions.

Dirty and I have the same interest in music, sports, and school. The only exception is Dirty is into hardcore heavy metal. Dirty never treats me differently because of my appearance due to having white friends in his neighborhood. He has a crush on my sister. I couldn't care less about his feelings for her. He is a cool dude. If Dirty wants to pursue my sister, I am okay with it.

Telly and Red start hanging out regularly. Telly is also fascinated with the gangs, drug life, and the hip-hop culture. Red starts to venture out more in the neighborhood. Days often pass before seeing him out. Not seeing him does not bother me because of my workload from school, practicing golf, and baseball. When I have free time, I want to watch TV when I get home. My sister is at a middle school close to where my mother works, so I enjoy being at home alone, even if it is for a couple of hours.

Once spring rolls around, Red starts bringing more guys to the neighborhood to play basketball at my house. I like the new competition, but it starts to become bothersome. I love having a golf lesson, baseball practice, or going to my aunt's house to practice golf to avoid playing basketball. It gets to the point where I ignore the doorbell if I am at home. Red will try to yell out obscenities under my window to see if he can get my attention. Red knows how I feel about my ethic makeup. He will try to trigger a nerve by calling me 'Dirty White Boy' if I do not answer. The obscenities do not bother me at all. I purposely ignore him when he resorts to these tactics.

My mother has a tall iron fence put up during the summer. The only way to enter is through the gate which requires a key to unlock. Red tries to con me on occasions to keep the gate unlocked, but I make sure it is secure before going in the house every evening. Telly starts joining Red, selling my house as the neighborhood basketball court when my mother has the court paved with concrete. I know some of the guys they bring from school, but some of these guys are complete strangers. They both think they have a personal gym they can use at their own freewill.

One afternoon, Telly and Red's new friends show up to play some ball. It is nice out, so I do not have an issue playing. These guys do not have respect for the rules I put in place. Red knows these are my mother's rules, but he tells me to slack up a bit. For whatever reason, Red is trying to impress these guys. Before one kid starts to play, he pulls off his jacket

56

to reveal a gun in a holster and places it on the outside AC unit. I am not sure it is real, but it looks legit enough from a distance.

Another kid unloads his pockets with a huge knot of cash, some brown vials, and some white tic-tac looking candy in a Ziploc bag. I quickly realize these guys must leave. I am not afraid of them. However, I am afraid of my mother seeing this stuff back here when she gets home from work. These guys are some minor league dope boys trying to make a name on the street. Red and Telly are trying to ride their coattails. I quickly snatch up the ball and tell them to leave.

"Do you want a bump to chill out a bit?" one of the strangers asks.

"A bump of what?" I yell back.

He is referring to the cocaine in the brown vials.

"Damn, Homer! You need to chill out." Red whispers to me.

"Why did you bring these guys to my house? You know my mother's rules, Red." I yell at the top of my lungs.

To show he is in complete control, Red grabs my shirt to back me up against a brick wall separating an elevated flowerbed from the patio.

"I said, chill out Homer!"

"Okay, Red!" I softly whisper for Red to turn me loose.

As soon as Red lets me go, I chuck the basketball in his face, which ignites a huge brawl.

Red and I fight all over the backyard. We are hitting each other with sticks, the rocks in the flowerbed, and fallen pinecones in the grass. The tide shifts in Red's favor when he hits me in the face with an iron lawn chair. Whatever he hits me with is not fazing me because all I can think about is my mother coming in the backyard and seeing the drugs and the gun. Telly eventually breaks us up because I am bleeding profusely from my nose. Red immediately motions to the guys to leave so they can find somewhere else to play ball. Telly hangs back for a moment to see if I am okay. I am fine but still visibly angry.

"The blow from the chair is how he got the drop on me." I express to Telly while pressing my shirt against my bloody nose.

"Don't worry, you got in some good blows. You guys were going toe to toe before he hit you with the chair." Telly states while laughing.

One of the guys quickly summons Telly to come on so they can leave. Telly being Telly, he starts to walk to the gate and laughs while telling me, "Well, I will see you tomorrow."

"As always." I reply laughing.

I do not mind taking the loss in the fight because I know my mother will kick the dog shit out of me if she comes home and discovers drugs and a gun on her property.

It is the weekend before I see Red again. Since I am tall enough to stand over the top bar of the lawnmower, I am responsible for cutting the grass. Red notices me in the yard. He comes over and starts talking as though nothing happened a few days earlier.

"Did you forget about what happened the other day?"

"What did I do?" Red asks with confusion.

Red has no recollection about our fight as he starts helping me gather the loose grass clippings. Red's intention is to get me done sooner so he can play basketball. I do not say much to him. Even though I appreciate the help, I am on guard just in case Red is using forgetfulness to seek revenge.

Once I finish, I sit on the back patio, looking over the yard admiring my work. I am still new to cutting grass and I want to make sure I am mowing it right. While watching Red shoot around, I conclude he had to be under the influence of one of the drugs the guys were carrying during our clash. This is the only way Red cannot remember our battle. Red begs me to join him in one-on-one, but I am too tired to play. To shut him up, I play him because it is about to rain. His intent is to beat me while I am on my 'A' game. I am playing lazy, and he is not happy about it. He calls me every derogatory name he can to get me to play him harder. The best thing happens when a rain drop hits my arm.

"I will see you after the rain stops."

"Homer, I do not have anywhere to go. I was supposed to go with my grandmother, but she left me when I didn't come home on time. She locked me out."

I reluctantly let him come in the house and things go back to normal despite the fact we both tried to beat each other's brains outs a few days ago.

Hole 7 – New Scrutiny

We get some new faces on our street during this time. Tee moves in a few houses down. He is about three years younger than us, but Tee is mature enough to hang out with guys in our age group. I quickly take a liking to Tee and bring him under my wing to make sure he is not bothered around the neighborhood. Tee is fortunate enough to attend an elementary school outside of our district. This way he can stay under the radar to avoid any potential trouble. Boom, Brigg's younger brother, moves in with his grandmother in the cove at the end of my street. Boom is funny for a young kid. He carries around a small handheld radio. His has the ambition of becoming the next Russell Simmons after watching the movie *Krush Grove* about a hundred times. He always tries to make a demo tape by transforming any type of noise into a beat to rhyme over. Cam moves in with his aunt and uncle after his parents died right across the street from Boom's grandmother's house. Que moves in with his grandmother across the street from my house after his mom passes away. Que is a talented kid but is troubled because he cannot cope with the death of his mom. Carl, Jesus, and C.J. live with their grandparents at the top of street right next to Free's aunt's house. These guys are cousins and smartly travel together to thwart away trouble. Jesus is the sensible one out of all three. He makes sure they stay away from the gang activity overflowing in the area. Ed moves into a house in the center of the cove. Ed is extremely bright, artistic, and a good athlete. I am not sure what type of activities takes place in his household, but Ed lashes out at authority. In my eyes, he is a smaller version of Red. Red latches on to C.J. and Que because the lure of the street life becomes a fascination for the three. In all fairness to Red, his intentions are not to sway them in a negative direction. All three love basketball, but the guys Red hangs around with heavily influence C.J. and Que. Jesus and I are pretty good friends, but C.J. and I do not hit it off well. C.J. is under the impression I am an instigator who causes trouble amongst himself, Boom, Tee, Que, Ed, and Cam. C.J. and Ed do not like each other at all. They fight on numerous occasions. Due to their ages, I look out for them to make sure they do not get influenced by the pool of negativity swimming around our neighborhood.

A friendly street rivalry develops between C.J., Jesus, and Carl on the west side of the street and Tee, Ed, and Que on the east side of the street. Boom often sits on the sidelines with Red and me acting as though he is a disc jockey. They compete in everything from baseball, football, basketball, racing bikes, and even stick fights in the woods. This fuels Red's and mine competitive juices because we join in against each other for bragging rights between ourselves. Tee and C.J. eventually get basketball goals in their yards, but it will be a year or so before the games transition from my house. My house is still the local gathering spot because I have the concrete court centrally located on the street. Because of the violent nature and the negativity of the schoolyard football games, I will not let these guys compete because they will get hurt.

The friendly rivalry between the two apartment complexes is turning ugly. It seems more fights are breaking out rather than playing football games. Some of the guys get high before the games. The only reason some of these guys

are playing is to hurt someone. Since I made a reputation
for myself on the field and after Dirty's retaliation, I am
growing tired of the cheap shots, the bruises, and scars.
Brute is becoming a less frequent visitor because he is now a
major player in the drug game, causing the football games to
become less of a priority. Without Brute there to keep things
in line, everything is spinning out of control. There are many
games where I fight more than play football. The more I fight,
the more the sin of rage fuels my thought process. I am afraid
I am about to hurt someone. Fortunately, a neighbor who
lives across the street from the elementary school grows tired
of our gatherings. These guys leave trash and walk all over
her manicured yard. She eventually picks up on the gang and
drug activity. Soon, the police are patrolling the schoolyard
while we play. It only takes two games for the police to show
up before the games are not organized for a while. This
stoppage does not bother me at all.

A neighbor who is a little older than Briggs, Slick,
and Hamp used to babysit my sister and me when we were
toddlers. At the time, she was the most beautiful girl I had
ever seen. A lot of guys try to court her, including one of my
older cousins. She starts dating a gentleman named Dre', who
drives the coolest two-seat tan Fiat. Dre' is smooth; he is the
definition of what the hood guys call preppy. Dre' wears the
dress slacks with the fresh loafers, and the distinguished sport
coats. When I see him for the first time, I tell myself this is
how I will represent myself when I am Dre's age. I get up the
nerve to talk to him one day and we hit it off immediately.
On this day, he's wearing his fraternity shirt. This sparks a
deep discussion about the organization.

"Will I be able to join once I get to college?" I ask.

"It depends. Many are called but only a few are
chosen. You shouldn't have any problems if you meet the
qualifications." Dre' responds with a smirk.

"You can see what my shortcomings are Dre'. Will an African American fraternity accept someone who looks like me?"

"Homer, just be you and you will make it anywhere in any environment."

After our discussion, I know this is the fraternity I want to pledge if I enroll in college. From this point on, Dre' always converses with me for a minute or two when he is picking up my neighbor. Our talks and his advice plant a seed, which will eventually take root and surfaces in a few years. However, I am still in the now, trying to figure out my place in this flower garden being choked out by weeds.

My confidence is high going into the summer. I graduate from the sixth grade in the top ten of my class, I discover my hormones, and I am going to middle school where my sister attends in the fall. This means I do not have to deal with the same classmates since kindergarten. I will meet a different set of kids with similar interests.

I participate in a few golf tournaments in the spring and win my first tournament. My baseball season is also wrapping up. My mother enrolls us in swimming lessons at a summer camp where most of the kids are Caucasian. Just like the golf clinics and tournaments, the white kids sense something unusual about my ethnic background. They know I am not one of them, but they cannot put a finger on my ethnic origin. This does not bother me as long as they do not want to physically express their concerns.

After three days of feeling out the environment, I settle in with the outcasts in my age group. They are a little weird. Yeah, right, like I can classify someone as weird! The camp is structured as though we are at a country campsite with outdoor activities. We compete against the so-called cool kids in all activities from tug of war, the obstacle course, and a game of leapfrog. The leapfrog games are the most intense. This game consists of jumping the distance of two sticks from a running start until there is only one group standing. The kids at the summer camp are just as malicious as some of the guys I encountered in my neighborhood. They talk plenty of noise and sometimes use dirty tactics to get a competitive advantage. Of course, this causes my competitive juices to flow. I inadvertently intimidate some of the guys in my circle because I desperately want to win. None of them want to be the one who causes us to lose for fear I may come down on them in a harsh manner. I am doing everything at one hundred miles per hour. All I want for my group is to compete at one hundred percent and not let the other group intimidate them because they are the more athletic group.

After the first loss we suffer at tug of war, I am fuming, causing my group to timidly stay out of my presence during lunch. The other group notices how I always compete on a high level. During lunch, they decide to approach me with a proposition.

"Homer, we are checking to see if you want to join the winning side. We know you are tired of losing all the time."

I remember looking over to my group, noticing the look on their faces. I can tell by their expressions they know I am going to accept the invitation.

"No thanks, guys." I politely reply.

"Why? Do you like being with those losers?"

My answer is straight forward, "Yes, I do like those losers. See, you guys treated me like I was below you in class because you couldn't figure out my racial makeup. All you had to do was ask and I would have told you. Then maybe we could have started a friendship. Instead, I am looking forward to kicking your asses in every event."

A few of them are stunned by my response. A couple of them threw back some derogatory hand gestures as I laugh, walking towards my group to eat.

As I sit down to finish eating, the guys around me are a little quiet.

"I don't mind losing, but I do mind if you are not trying." I state to break the silence.

Another kid chimes in to give validation to my remarks. After this incident, the rest of the four-week camp is enjoyable. We do not win every game or event, but we put up a hell of a fight against the other boys. I probably would not have the confidence I have now if I backed down from all the confrontations or challenges I faced in my neighborhood. Maybe growing up an outcast in Alcy is the reason God placed me in this environment. The advice on confidence from my grandmother and Dre' telling me to be myself is constantly repeating in my mind.

There are girls in our age group attending the camp. They are too prissy for my taste. During this time, I realize I am not attracted to blond, blue-eyed women. I am growing up around young black girls in my community. They are my predilection due to the curves of their bodies, being feisty, and their assertiveness. The shade of the skin does not matter if they are appealing to the eye. There are no women on Earth like women of color. In my eyes, they are God's true image of a woman.

Even though I am having fun at summer camp and with the new group of guys in the neighborhood, I am anticipating seeing my grandparents. Once we arrive, I wait a few days before telling them everything I experienced and learned this year to let my sister get everything out of her system. My sister let it slip out to my grandfather she is interested in boys. I think my grandfather is still preaching to her about guarding her chastity belt. My grandfather is very candid to my sister about boys' intentions. I get a kick out of watching my sister get frustrated because she cannot formulate a rebuttal to my grandfather's arguments. My grandmother often snickers under her breath as we both sit back shelling butter beans and picking greens during some of the debates. Both of us are very entertained by their arguments.

One late night, my grandfather decides to go the grocery store. This is just how he shops. He does not like being around a crowd of people. I am still up, looking at my newly purchased baseball cards when he asks me if I want to ride along. I do not hesitate because I always enjoy spending time with him regardless of the destination. On the way, he asks me about the school year. I immediately tell him everything. I do not hold back. I tell him about my work in school, the computer lab, the trip with my aunt, the gangs, the fight with Red, how I discovered my hormones, and kissing Free and Ally.

"How did you feel while you were kissing them Homer?"

"I got a little confused when I started to get a funny feeling in my private area."

"Did you talk to your mother about how you felt?"

"No, I thought she would freak out. Plus, I was a little embarrassed. I wanted to reach out to my father, but I was afraid." I state as I turn my head to look out the car window.

"Why?" my grandfather asks.

"I was afraid he wouldn't talk to me." I respond with a tear streaming from my eye.

My grandfather then starts to give me the talk about the birds and the bees. At first, he is getting too technical with scientific terms and definitions. I ask him to bring it down to a sixth-grade level. He laughs and keeps explaining while we walk down every aisle in the grocery store. Even though the topic is about sex, he is not talking quietly. Some of the night stockers and shoppers are taken back a bit when we pass by with our discussion.

"Sex is a beautiful experience. One day, you will meet the one girl who will make you release your pollen into her flower. Now listen closely to this, Homer. Everything that looks good to you is not good for you. Make sure you watch out for the aggressive ones." My grandfather states passionately.

I am soaking in everything he is explaining. I also tell my grandfather about what some of the guys are saying in school about sex.

"What they are telling you and learning is wrong!" My grandfather yells.

"I thought so, but their stories are quite entertaining."

"The stories get even better when you talk to old dudes like me." He states with a chuckle.

When I look at the clock in the car on the way home, it is well past one in the morning. We are still talking as we unload the car and put away the groceries. I always feel I can tell my grandfather anything. I call him weekly to discuss anything on my mind.

This particular summer, my uncle moves back home from living out of town. He gets a job as a community center director. He tells my grandmother that my sister and I can go to work with him every day instead of just sitting around the house. My uncle always makes sure we are entertained because he is a party animal and loves to have fun. He entertains us Monday through Friday, but he goes out of town every weekend to see his boyfriend. I think he wants to hide he is gay from my sister and I, but we do not care. My uncle treats us like his niece and nephew, and this is all that matters to us.

Unfortunately, his community center is located on a rough street. The building is new, but the environment is horrible. The neighborhood surroundings do not matter to me because it looks like some areas of Memphis. My initial impression is to transform into my back home mode to prepare for the stares, stereotypes, and altercations. These kids are growing up rough, but they are not any different from the kids back home. I am happy to say over a four-week period, I only have one altercation. It is a misunderstanding, which is quickly resolved before it gets out of hand.

Most of the boys want to play basketball all day. I am at the point where I am getting fed up with the game. My sister is having a ball because boys are giving her all types of attention. I am growing tired of folks thinking we are from a small country town. Our metropolitan area is close to eight hundred thousand people. This town barely has twenty-five thousand. My other uncle, the popular football coach at the high school, works part time in the parks during the summer. During his site visits, some kids cannot understand how I am his nephew because we have different skin complexions. I come to the realization part of our growth as a people is inhibited by our inability to have an open mind mixed with a lack of knowledge of the history of the evolution of African Americans in the United States.

I do not have any issues with the girls in camp. They are fascinated with my hair and eyes. One girl comes on a little too strong while I am putting some equipment in an upstairs utility closet at the request from my uncle. I notice her in the camp, flirting with the other boys. She is very advanced for her age. I can tell she feels she has to come on strong to boys to get their attention. From the way her body is developed, she looks as though she is in her late teens. Guys only think of her as an immediate cure to their raging hormones. She has a cute face, but most of the attention she receives is because of her body.

She closes the door to the utility room and blocks me from the exit. She has a couple of her friends block the stairway to signal if anyone is coming to avoid interrupting her intentions.

"What are you doing?" I ask kindly as she begins to remove her blouse.

I do not have time to analyze the situation because she presses me against the wall for us to start kissing. Now, this is one of those moments where you pause to think about what to do next. My body and curiosity are telling me to see where this may lead, but in a split second, my grandfather's advice quickly surfaces in my mind. Then other things, like not knowing this girl's name, pops in my head.

Where is the beauty in this? I ask myself.

With Free and Ally, I at least had a connection by knowing something about them.

"Can we slow down a bit?" I ask the girl.

"Oh, you want to be in control?" the girl states as she lays down on a broken pool table laying in the closet.

Once again, I am at a crossroad because my body and demons are saying 'go' but my mind is telling me to 'slow your role.' At this point, the body and demons are winning the race. However, the situation does not feel right.

The sin of lust almost takes over when she exposes her breasts and teases me with them in the closest.

"I know you want to play with these." The girl states to seduce me.

"I can't do this where we are located. If this is going to be something special, I at least want to know something about you or have an emotional connection with you. I don't even know your name."

The young lady is baffled and begins to reconfirm my gut instinct to not go any further.

"You are the first one who has turned this down. I have been with a lot of guys who have taken advantage of the moment." She states before going into a profanity tirade, calling me everything in the book for turning her down.

I am smiling during the verbal assault because my grandfather was right. Even though she looks good to me, she is not good for me due to being overly aggressive and having a horrible attitude. I know most guys in this circumstance will tell what I should have done. I am not worried about having a scoring title regarding girls just yet. I know the right one will come eventually.

I stopped going to camp because my grandparent's neighbor's grandkids were starting to make their way in from out of town. We play from sunup to sundown and often must be called in the house because it is so late. Our favorite sport was kickball, and we play each game like it was the World Series. These guys are also into skateboarding and freestyle biking. We go to the yearly tour of the freestyle skaters and bikers when they are in the Richmond area. I am mesmerized by the participants' style and swagger. They are wearing baggy shorts and t-shirts expressing their attitude and I quickly adapt to the laid-back style. The participants are talented guys, and we closely observe them as they perform their tricks for hours and hours.As soon as we are back home, we attempt to imitate what we just witnessed. I wish I can say we were ready for the X-games, but we look more like a blooper reel. We flip and fall all over the place. I flip myself off a bike while attempting to do a harrow trick off a ramp. I am surprised I don't seriously injure myself. We scar and scrape our bodies.

We leave a lot of skin on the concrete during this summer. Regardless of the injuries, we are having a blast.

We find a trail leading to a railroad track, which cuts through the town. We were amazed at the how close we are to the trains and their speed as they pass. We put bottles and rocks on the tracks to marvel how the trains demolish these objects. We also discover the Amtrak passenger trains release human waste directly on the tracks. We can also determine how far away a train is from our location by the vibrations on the track. With some of the stuff we put on the track, I am surprised we do not derail a train.

My grandmother has a neighbor who lives directly behind her who encourages my sister and I to visit. She makes the best tuna fish. Her daughter is about my uncle's age, and she takes us out at least one time during the summer. This young lady eventually marries, and my grandparent's neighbor inherits a step-grandson named Ant who is about our age. Now, this guy is a piece of work. For him to be our age, Ant has already developed the mindset women are inferior to men. Of course, Ant and my sister do not mesh well at all. He was spoiled growing up and his father has sole custody after their divorce. Ant joins our circle during the day and quickly makes enemies from the start. Ant wants to prove to everyone he is the best at everything. This is the type of kid who doesn't have much interaction with others his age, so the best way for him to make friends is to try to impress everyone. We tolerate him at first, but he eventually becomes a pain. My sister joins us on occasions, only because she and another guy, Ron, are sweet on each other.

One day, we are at the school park playing stick ball. The teams consist of myself, Ant, Ron, and my sister playing against the other guys in the circle. We are losing and Ant's philosophy is because we are playing with a girl. I warn him to back off a bit because I am the only one who can put down my sister, only because I feel this is my job due to being siblings. My sister ignores him and continues her style of play. She isn't doing a bad job and we are only down a few runs. During the previous inning, we cut into the lead on offense and looking to make a stand on defense to take the lead during our next at bat.

While getting set on defense, Ant is mouthing off to my sister, telling her we can do better on offense if she quits making mistakes. While hearing him talk to her, I can't remember the mistakes he is referencing. Once again, I ask him to back off her, which causes things to escalate into a minuscule shoving match.

We are playing underhand pitching and Ron designates my sister as the pitcher so the rest of us can play defense. The other team starts to get on a roll and expanded their lead. Ant is furious and decides he will pitch to get us out of the inning. Ant approaches the mound and snatches the ball from my sister with the upmost lack of respect. I immediately take off to the mound to let him know he will not disrespect my sister this way. In my peripheral vision, I see Ron rush past me to confront Ant on the mound. Ant angrily pushes Ron back. I don't know when Ron had time to pick up a dried-up piece of wood, but he clocks Ant across his head. The wood is so dried up it explodes as soon as it makes contact. Ant is in such shock; he immediately takes off to his grandmother's house. We all sit back to let the incident settle in for a moment. We all look at each other and fall into a hilarious laughter. Ant is so hurt; he calls his stepmother and leaves during the evening. We do not see him again until the following summer.

Ron's folks invite my sister and me to go to their family reunion at a campsite about an hour away. For the way we are as kids, this is a like being in a candy store. They have archery, zip lines, and canoeing. Me, Ron, and Ron's little brother decide to take an adventure in the canoe.

We row all over the lake and come upon a small island. We hike every square inch of the land just being curious. Ron's little brother discovers the biggest beehive we have ever seen. It is so big; we can hear the bee's buzzing about thirty yards away. Ron decides he wants a closer look. I have watched too many natural geographic specials on bees to join him. Ron's little brother and I decide to head back to the canoe while Ron plays Jacques Cousteau. I don't know what he does but he disrupts the hive because we hear the bees get louder as we are getting on the canoe. Ron rushes onto the boat and tells us to paddle with everything we have. You would have thought the bees were right behind us, but they only sent a few bees Ron's way to back him off. Once we'd paddled to the middle of the lake, we look back and laugh. It is almost getting dark, so we head back to the campsite to leave for home.

We are leaving in a few days. Honestly, I do not want the summer to end. On the flip side, I am excited about experiencing new things this school year. My grandfather accompanies us on our trip home because the airline no longer offers a direct flight from Richmond to Memphis. Home always looks different when you have been gone for a while. I always go to my room when I return to lie around looking at the walls. I am soaking in the summer activities when Red suddenly appears in my room. He is not alone because I can hear the ball bouncing in the backyard. Damn, can I get settled in before getting asked to play basketball? Dirty is practicing his shooting, waiting on us to come out. Red is filling me in on what is going on in the neighborhood while squeezing in questions about my summer happenings. I do not tell him everything. I am not about to mention what happened in the utility closet. I don't want to listen to the ridicule or hear Red go on and on about what he would do if he was in this situation.

As I make my way to the court and start shooting, I hear a huge crack. Dirty is startled by the sound and asks me to shoot the ball again. After the ball hits the goal, the rim comes crashing down. My grandfather observes the incident in total disbelief. After he inspects everything, he grabs the rim so we can return the defective net to the department store.

"Someone was definitely dunking in order for the rim to collapse, causing the damage." The salesman tells my grandfather.

"The goal is too high for my grandson to dunk. Plus, he just arrived back home from being out of town. Why don't you ask my grandson about the incident?"

The gentleman has a confused look on his face.

"Where is your grandson?" The salesman asks.

"Right here!" My grandfather states while pointing to me standing next to him.

"I don't see him." The salesman says while looking around the counter.

I am standing right beside my grandfather. The gentlemen cannot believe my grandfather could have a Caucasian-looking grandson.

This is how the summer went this year. It was full of the unexpected and long-lasting lifetime memories. School is ready to start in a few days, marking the end of another season. I am anticipating a new beginning, but unaware of what I am about to battle.

Hole 8 – Confidence Shattered

Summer is over and it is off to Middle School. My school offers a college preparatory program for kids who live outside the school's residency requirement zone. I am a little restless the night before because I am not sure what to expect. Immediately after arriving, I see a familiar face. A kid named Silver; I recognize as an observer at some of our neighborhood football games. Silver's aunt is the neighbor who phoned the police because of the suspicious activities and the guys trashing her yard. We quickly notice each other but we reintroduce ourselves. We did not talk much when he was at his aunt's house. We quickly latch onto each other and talk as we head to the auditorium to get our homeroom assignments.

Because the program is open to all, I attend school with a mixture of cultures. Most of the population is African American, but there are also Caucasian, Middle Eastern, and Asian kids sprinkled into the mix. The downside is we attend school with the neighborhood kids who live in the housing projects within walking distance. This does not bother me for the first few days. But after a couple of days, I realize I need to revert to the defense mechanisms I learned in elementary school. These students define us as uppity or preppy because we are in a college preparatory curriculum.

I am taking my time walking to my homeroom because I am trying to figure out the room numbers and observe the construction of the building. The building is old. You can tell the school board is cutting corners on the maintenance. There are water spots on the ceilings, tiles missing in the floor, and the lockers look like they are coated with fresh paint to look new. When I walk into my homeroom, I am greeted by a lively spirit of a teacher. Ms. Loper is an English teacher who has been teaching for a long time. She seems pleasant and her liveliness helps to ease the tension of the first day jitters. A couple of people try to take her vivacious personality as a sign of weakness, but Ms. Loper quickly lets them know who is in control. Ms. Loper encourages us to get to know each other while she hands out schedules and locker assignments. Most of the kids, who already know each other from the neighborhood, gravitate to form different cliques. Ms. Loper quickly breaks this up by asking who in the class already knows each other. I do not know anyone. I am not comfortable letting my defenses down to meet others just yet. I feel I will let things happen instead of trying to push myself on others. Honestly, I am a little guarded—not wanting others to know anything about my ethnic background due to some of the incidents I experienced while in elementary school. Ms. Loper forces us to introduce ourselves and sit next to someone we do not know.

"You will be together for the next three years so it will be to your advantage to get to know each other." Ms. Loper orders to a silent room.

I deliberately shut myself off from my classmates as I skim over my schedule as the other kids discuss their schedules aloud. Four of the six classes on my schedule are honors classes. Gym and art are the only classes not classified as accelerated. I receive a bottom locker for the school year. This is a problem because of my height. I am beginning to have growing pains in my knees and waist. I must bend or squat down to turn my combination to unlock the locker. So far, I am not enjoying the middle school experience.

Little things occur chipping away at my confidence. During the first week of gym class, we are given fitness assessments to measure our flexibility, endurance, and timed in a mile run. The mile run consists of four laps around the field located at the rear of our school. I tell myself this task shouldn't be tough because of the distances I run during the schoolyard football games and the basketball games at home. I run with a classmate, so we are in sync with our time. Once we are on the last lap, we ease up because we know we will post a good time.

"No, sir, you are not finished! You still owe me one more lap." My gym teacher yells.

"I did four laps." I state, pleading my case.

"Yes, he did because we ran them together." My classmate exclaims.

"I watched you the entire time and I only counted three laps."

Instead of posting a time of about five and a half minutes, my time is documented a little less than eight minutes because of the minute or so I spend debating with my gym teacher. For the entire semester, she continues to over analyze and knit pick everything I do during class. Even in wiffle ball, she tells me I am putting too much spin on the ball while I am pitching. Dang, a whiffle ball can't help but spin when it is thrown. She assists the basketball coach during tryouts. When I see her in the gym as I come out of the locker room, I know my tryout will not last long. I am not saying I should have made the team, but I play well enough to at least make the first or second cut. I am baffled as to why she dislikes me. Her ridiculing and chastising are the jumpstart of my slide into obscurity.

On some days, I take the city bus home. Public transportation is entertaining and provides some comic relief after a long day at school. There are all types of people on the bus. You have the hardworking people who just got off work from the hospital close to the school, the dirty old men who seem to get a kick out of watching the young girls on the bus, and the winos using the bus as a resting spot after a drinking binge. I particularly like the folks who start preaching or dishing out philosophy to anyone who listens. They go on and on until folks on the bus start giving them money to shut up. Most of the kids, who <u>have</u> to use this means of transportation, typically start out on the same bus. We all branch out to take different transfers about three or four miles south of our school. I vividly remember my bus route. I take either the '13' or the '20' bus to transfer to the number '4', which drops me off across the road from my elementary school. From here, it is about a five-minute walk home.

One day at the bus stop, I hear this one kid's voice over the fifty or so kids waiting for the bus. The voice is loud and keeps getting louder as everyone in the crowd elevates their voices to drown this kid out. This kid is just joking around, playing with the girls, and trying to sell peanut M&M's.

His catchphrase is, "I got the nuts!"

"Hey, white dude! You want some of these nuts?" The voice blurts out as he gets closer to me.

I laugh at his sales pitch and purchase a box for fifty cents. He introduces himself as Gold. I am thrown off a bit by his name. Gold provides the history behind his name. Gold is a sharp kid, but it takes him until the ninth grade to get my last name right. He always refers to me as the 'white boy' in the crowd. I keep my eye on Gold because I am not sure of his intentions. I stupidly characterized him with the guys in my neighborhood I eventually fought who classify me this way. I always get enraged when someone references me this way without getting to know who I am as person.

I receive criticism from the guys in my neighborhood about going to a preppy middle school. There are only a few differences between my school and the one they are attending. Because I am in Honors classes, a fair amount of homework is assigned each night. On the days the homework is light; I go home and chill out for the evening or practice something in relation to golf in the backyard. My body is hurting from the growing pains I am experiencing, causing me to sleep and eat more. I can take a nap in the afternoon, get up and eat dinner, and go back to sleep at about nine o'clock. I do not see much of Red, Grey, and Telly. When I do, they give me an earful about me turning into an uppity preppy know-it- all while forgetting where I come from because I go to a different school. I constantly explain to them this is not the case. I am the same person they have known for years. I love when Dirty is around when they start to get on my case.

Dirty tells them to, "Back off" or, "Shut it up! Can't you see he is trying to do something with himself?"

Dirty is in the same Honors program at another school and can relate to the academic stress.

I limit my basketball and outdoor activities to the weekend so I can focus on schoolwork and golf. I begin to sleep in on Saturdays. If I go outside, I make my appearance after lunch. Red is not thrilled about this, so he starts to spend more time at C.J.'s and Jesus' house to practice his basketball skills. When we have games at my house, Red and Telly are starting to bring more and more guys to play. There are enough individuals to play three-on-three, then more start showing up to where it becomes four-on-four. Once you get to four-on-four, you really need to play full court ball at a park.

I am at the age where my mother leaves me at home while she is out running errands. To get out of playing ball on some Saturday's, I often tell Red I must go with my mother. I then go straight to my room until she returns. I am annoyed with the amount of people because some of them do not respect the backyard rules. For a few weeks, I notice no one is showing up to play. Boom tells me C.J. has moved his goal into their backyard to accommodate more people for pickup games. I am so relieved I run up to their house to watch the games. I do not want to play. I just sat back and watch C.J. and Jesus handle the stress that comes with having a basketball goal in your yard.

One weekday evening, Red, Dirty, and I are playing three-on-three with some guys Red brought over to the house for a game. I sense trouble from the beginning because I fought two of these guys during some of the schoolyard football games. I remember Dirty slamming one of these guys to the concrete when they tried to tackle him on the sideline. These guys are good, but the three of us are giving them some good competition. Red is having an off day due to how his defender is playing his game. This guy is like glue on Red. He figures out he can pressure Red all game to force the offense to go through either Dirty or myself. Dirty and I try to set screens to free up Red so he can have open looks at the net. The defender knows how to move through the screens, which allows him to eliminate our attempt to give Red an offensive advantage. Even though they beat us four out of the seven games we play, they are some good close games.

Red is frustrated and begins mouthing off to his defender once they are about to go home for the evening. This guy does not allow Red to mouth off at him, so he rushes over and punches him. The punch does not affect Red as he retaliates and the two begin to fight in my driveway. Dirty jumps in to assist because Red is his cousin. This causes the other two guys to jump in to assist their comrade. I try to break up the altercation, but I am forced to the ground because it looks as though I am jumping in to assist Red and Dirty. This fight quickly turns ugly when Dirty is one-on-one with his foe. The bigger guy fighting Dirty shifts his attention on me, and I struggle trying to fight this guy. Red is also struggling with his bigger opponent. This leaves Dirty with a smaller adversary. He makes this guy pay for getting involved in the mayhem. Dirty choke slams the guy into my neighbor's trash can. He then easily slams him headfirst into the RV parked in the same neighbor's yard. This opens a huge gash on this kid's head leaving a dent on the side of the RV. The kid lets out a huge cry, which diverts my foe's attention for a split second. The distraction allows me to get the upper hand to get this goliath of a kid off me. Simultaneously, Dirty rushes over to assist Red while my foe goes to check on his friend. Red's opponent does not want anything to do with the two and quickly fades back to where his friends are gathered by the RV.

The gash is bad. From my view, I am sure the kid needs stitches. I feel bad so I try to offer some help to the guy. Red, Dirty, and our three enemies all give me a look of confusion when I run in the storage room and grab a car wash towel so he can apply pressure to the wound. One of the guys grabs the towel with hostility and puts it on the kid's head as they abruptly make their way back to wherever they live. I can tell by the look they give us as they walk off this battle is far from over. The neighbor who owns the RV quickly runs out and escorts Dirty and Red home so he can tell their grandmother about the damage to his RV. I sit on the front porch for a while because I know my neighbor is coming over to my house next to tell my mother about the fight. My neighbor does not show, so I go in for the night. I have trouble sleeping because I am worried if the injured kid is okay. I also wonder what type of retaliation these guys are planning.

The next day at school, a group of us are playing touch football on the field at the rear of the school during lunch. When the ball is thrown in my direction, I catch it and make a slight cut up field. While making the cut, I lose my footing a but while attempting to spin off the defender. As I clumsily make the spin, I unintentionally elbow a kid in the face while he is approaching me from behind. The kid I spin away from makes the tag, stopping my forward momentum. When I stop, the kid I accidentally hit confronts me about the elbow to the face.

"Man, why did you do that?" The kid angrily states.

"It was an accident. I couldn't control my momentum when I did the spin move."

"I think it was on purpose." The kid replies with his fists prepared for a duel.

"Man, I don't want to fight you." I state somberly.

After witnessing the injury to the guy's head on yesterday, I am done fighting. I figure it is time to learn how to negotiate my way out of confrontations. Silver is standing close to me on the field while I am trying to defuse the situation. Before I can say anything else, this kid hits me with two solid punches to the face. I am enraged, so I attempt to strike back. Before I can do anything, the school's resource officer pulls me away from the kid.

The officer quickly escorts us to the principal's office. The officer reports the incident as a racial hate crime to the secretary.

"The black kid was beating up on the white kid." The officer tells the secretary.

I am floored because the resource officer intervened in after my foe connected two punches. I didn't get a chance to retaliate. To make matters worse, the principal gives me the highest form of punishment below expulsion. I am given a suspension requiring a board committee's approval before I can come back to school.

"It was an accident. The elbow was not intentional. I did a spin move and lost my footing. He ran into my elbow while chasing me from behind. I don't understand why I am being severely punished. He threw two punches. I didn't get a chance to swing back."

"The elbow equates to a punch, which initiated the other kid to react in the manner of throwing his two punches. Your punishment is based on the Board of Education guidelines. I am strictly following the rules." My principal explains.

By this time, my mother arrives wanting a detailed explanation. At first, the principal is short and evasive, but quickly realizes my mother requires answers with more detail due to the questions being asked. My mother is a paralegal at a law firm. She is used to asking questions to get to the truth of the subject matter. As I try to get a few words in about my unjust punishment, I am quickly told to be quiet.

In the end, my principal does not give in to changing the type of suspension. By the time I go to my math class to get my belongings, the news of the fight has spread across the kids in my grade. Two punches quickly turn into an all-out assault. Stories surface how I am beaten to a pulp. The memory of what happened to me in third grade enters my mind. Will other people come after me because they think I am a punching bag? Will I have to prove myself over and over to show I am not a push over? This is a road I do not want to travel again.

After returning to school from my suspension, I am ridiculed a bit. A couple of days later, another fight breaks out in the cafeteria. This diverts the attention away from my altercation. The kid who punched me, and I make amends a few days later. However, I am still skeptical about those around me at school. I am even more cynical about running into the three guys we fought while walking home.

Hole 9 – Blind-Sided

Slick helps me out some days by picking me up from school when he does not have an afternoon class. He helps me with my math and science since he is strong in these subject areas. If I do well on an assignment, Slick lets me tinker around with some games on his computer. Slick's computer is top of the line for the mid-80s. It has multiple hard drives, the phone to link up with other computers, and the top-of-the-line color monitor.

Slick tells us his computer has the capacity to film a movie. Slick often mentions he is considering doing a documentary on the kids in the neighborhood. After one study session in Slick's room, he asks me to crank up his computer so he can show me what he has already filmed. He gives me a disk to load in the hard drive. Once the file is loaded, I can sense something is not right by the graphic images showing on the screen. I think I am seeing a mirage and rub my eyes to make sure the images are real. After taking a moment to digest what is happening, I know what is about to happen next is not good.

"Do you like what is on the screen?" Slick asks while stroking my hair.

Now this does not feel good at all. I know I am not gay because the feeling I get when a girl stokes my hair is a lot different from a man's touch. I need to do something to get out of this situation as fast as possible. I slow down the situation in my mind by trying to find a way out of his room. His room is on the second floor, so going out the window is out.

"Man, I need to go to the restroom!" I reply with fear in my tone.

"In a minute, Homer! Just sit in the chair and relax."

Slick is blocking my path to the door. We are home alone so yelling is not an option. Due to being overloaded with fear, I jump out of the chair to make a dash to the door. I am immediately cut off by Slick as he slams me into the wall. Due to my altercations with larger guys, I always look around for something to use as a weapon to get control of my bigger opponent. However, I am out of luck because I cannot find anything in reach. I immediately take a swing to back him off me, but I am overpowered as Slick pins me to the floor on my back.

"Does this feel good?" Slick asks as he presses himself against me.

I cannot respond because I am in shock. We wrestle for a few more minutes. I am fighting back as hard as I can because Slick is trying to remove my clothes while we are tussling. The more I struggle, the more I feel him getting aroused. For a moment, I think I have a chance to escape when I knee him in his mid-section. Thinking I have a clear shot to the bedroom door, Slick grabs me from behind forcing me onto his bed on my stomach.

Fortunately, I hear his front door unlocking. The dead bolt turning is clear as day and startles Slick. I give him another knee to his mid-section before I immediately rise and take off out of his bedroom. Slick's mother leaves something at home preventing her from completing an errand. The house has split levels with the front door being on the middle level. As Slick's mother goes downstairs, I rush out the front door before it closes from her entering the house. I dart to my house, which is about a hundred yards away.

Upon entry, I realize I left my backpack in Slick's room. I think about how I will get my stuff because I am not going back over there ever again. Even though our skin never makes contact, I jump in the shower thinking the soap and water will wash away what Slick tried to do to me. I cry in the shower because I do not understand why someone would want to do something like this to me. I feel beyond low. I must have done something wrong to be treated this way. I want to tell someone, but I feel ashamed and embarrassed. I lock my bedroom door because I am at a point where I do not trust anyone.

Later in the night, I look out my bedroom window at Slick's house, wondering where are the people who should protect me. Would this have happened if my father was here? If I was of dark complexion, would Slick have tried to assault me? I feel alone. I wonder if this sick bastard stalked me and if he tried something like this with anyone else. All night, all kind of different scenarios dance through my mind. However, I always come back to the conclusion what happened to me is my fault because of the way I look.

The next day, I think about not going to school. However, I do not want my mother to notice something is wrong. If I do not go to school, I know my mother will ask Slick to look after me while she is at work.

When I leave for school, I notice my backpack is placed on the front porch. Only one person could have brought my backpack home. It is neatly arranged and organized. Slick is probably using this tactic as a peace offering in hopes of buying my silence. I am not going to say anything, but I will not allow peace between us. I am angry. My demons vow to me I will one day obtain revenge for his actions. The sin of wrath is planted in my heart.

For the next few weeks, I am in a complete slump. I cannot focus on anything. My schoolwork, athletics, and socializing are suffering because I feel terrible. I sleep for hours and hours to avoid being awake because I do not want to face anything in the outside world. I feel every human emotion except love. I feel everyone around me is meant to do me harm.

Dirty is still trying to court my sister. She told him something is wrong with me. He asks to talk to me when I feel better. I am on the front porch one Sunday morning when Red and Dirty stop by before heading somewhere to hang out for the day.

"Red, I will catch up you later. Homer! What is wrong with you? I saw you darting from Slick's a few weeks back, which is about the same time you have been in this funk." Dirty states with sincerity.

"If I tell you something, will you keep this between us? This is extremely personal. I can't have you ridiculing and joking around with me." I express with tears in my eyes because I think he is going to start teasing me.

"Sure, Homer. You have my word."

I know Dirty is sincere because your word is your only source of credibility in our environment. After getting confirmation from Dirty, I begin to spill everything to him on my front porch. Once I am finished, Dirty stands up, stretches, and sits right back down.

"Man, Slick and Hamp tried something like this on me a while back. Slick is where Red gets his distorted views on sex." Dirty confesses as he puts his arm on my shoulder.

"How did you manage to escape?"

I am floored as Dirty tells me every detail of how he managed to get away.

"He tried the same thing with Red. Red told me in confidence he freaked out when he was asked to crank up Slick's computer. He heard our grandmother call for him to come from across the street. He immediately took off running out of the house to answer her calling."

We both laugh because we know this is one of the few times Red has answered his grandmother's call for him to come home.

"Homer, how do you feel?" Dirty asks.

"Words cannot describe how I am feeling. I am angry because this is a guy my mother trusts, my grandfather adores, and I thought was a genuine friend."

"I think we both can agree your experience was the more horrific one. You need to get your mind off this for a while. Join us at C.J.'s house to play a little ball."

This is the last time Dirty and I hang out. Over the summer, Dirty is killed when he is hit in the back of the head with a bat during an altercation in his parent's neighborhood. I am out of town at my grandparent's house in Petersburg when I get the news. I cannot help but think the guys we fought after our basketball game are responsible for his death. My thoughts are also on Red. Red is at a point where he is doing right in school and listening to the adults in his life. Dirty is the key piece keeping him in line because he is highly influential on Red. I fear Dirty's death will stray him off the path he is on down a corridor to the dark side of life. My good friend Dirty was only thirteen years old.

After hearing of Dirty's death at my grandparent's house, the rest of the summer is sort of a blur. I cannot sleep at night because I keep replaying the events of the year over and over in my head. While lying in bed a couple of days before we are to return home, I wish for the plane to crash so I will not have to deal with Slick. I feel this predator defecating on my life every day since the incident. Regardless of how many times I try to wash away this incident, I feel unclean and unworthy in God's eyes. I sit up at night asking God why he would let someone attempt to do what Slick did to me. I mean, this guy stalked and made calculated moves to gain the trust from me and my mother. Slick spent years planning his assault.

During a sermon at my grandmother's church, the preacher states God loves everyone regardless of their sins. I get confused because I feel God does not love me for letting my friend die and almost being sexually assaulted. I keep wondering if God will forgive Slick's sin of lust. Suicide enters my mind as well, because I am driving myself crazy trying to figure out what I did wrong.

Once my sister and I return home, I peep out of my window for a moment towards Slick's house. Vivid flashbacks of what could have happened rush through my mind. While reminiscing on the incident in Slick's room, I see Red coming down the street. I immediately drop everything to go see him. Once I yell to him from my front porch, I can tell by his mannerisms he is having a hard time adjusting to life without Dirty.

"Do you want to play basketball?" I ask to get his full attention.

At first, Red is all for playing a game. After a few shots, Red loses interest.

"I must ask what happened the day Dirty died. Were the guys we fought responsible?" I ask after some small talk.

"No, Dirty had a long feud with a kid in his neighborhood. The day before he died, Dirty and this guy got into a bad fight over a girl. Apparently, what he did to this kid was worse than splitting the guy's head open on the

RV. Dirty beat the crap out of this guy. The next day, this guy follows Dirty and his friend home after spending the night at his friend's house. His killer jumps out from behind a tree and blind-sides him with a blow to the back of his head. Dirty's friend thinks he is next, so he runs. Once his friend notices the guy who hit Dirty takes off running in the opposite direction, he immediately goes to the closest house to call for help. Dirty is rushed to the hospital where he was on life support for three days before they removed him from the machine," Red explains with sadness.

"Did they arrest his killer?"

"He was arrested. The kid pleaded self-defense and waived his right to a trial to receive a diversion sentence. Since this kid is only fifteen, he can have the offense removed from his record if he stays arrest-free until he is twenty-one." Red answers.

As Red and I play ball, I notice he is wearing the latest brand of tennis shoes on the market.

"What's up with the new shoes, Red? When did you get them? Better yet, how did you get them?"

"Don't worry about it, Homer!" Red replies to blow me off.

Based on his response, I immediately know Red is involved in illegal activities.

Once we finish playing, Red asks me to walk to the store because he is a little nervous about walking by himself. While we walk, Red tells me to look over my shoulder when walking home from the bus stop after school. He is hearing rumors about the guys we fought retaliating against us. He has been doubtful about walking alone since Dirty's death. Red shows me the small handgun in his possession. The way my mentality is at this moment, I sincerely hope these guys will jump us to put me out of this misery.

On our way to the store, we run across Brute and his companion, Tike. Brute and I exchange pleasantries as Tike and I give each other a fist pound. We know each other from our elementary school days. I notice Brute is decked out in the latest trend of clothes, shoes, and jewelry. I give him complements on his look, but Brute cuts me off for a moment to pull Red aside for a conversation.

While Tike and I are catching up, I notice Brute giving Red a package and giving out vivid, precise instructions. I can tell Brute means business by the look in his eyes as he gives out the directives. Even though I cannot hear the conversation, I can tell whatever is in the package is serious business. Tike is questioning me about my school and heckling me about still playing golf and baseball. He starts out wanting to know about the girls. He then shifts his inquiries to the gangs at my school. Tike's focus is to see if I know who is running drugs through the school.

"Homer, I will pay you top dollar for this information." Tikes exclaims.

Brute hears the end of the conversation and quickly tells Tike to drop the subject. Brute and I pick up our conversation right where we left off before he pulled Red to the side.

"Are you having any problems at the preppy school of yours? You should fit right in playing golf and baseball." Brute asks with a chuckle. "Everything is fine where I am located."

"Are you two having some problems in the hood?" Brute asks Red and me as he transforms from joking to serious in the blink of an eye.

"We have one needing attention." I reply, as Red taps me on the arm to be quiet.

"That's what I like about you, Homer. You always tell the truth. I know the situation you are talking about. Don't worry about it anymore. We handled it for you."

"Huh?" I reply in confusion.

"I said not to worry about it. Everything is under control. I told you while I am around, no one will fuck with you. Do you need some money to go to the store?" Brute asks.

"No, I am good, but thanks anyway, Brute." I reply stunned.

We say our goodbyes and continue our journey.

"Hey, Red! Make sure you let Homer get whatever he wants from the store." Brute yells from about twenty yards away.

Red gives him a hand gesture letting Brute know he received the order.

"Are you a runner for Brute?" I ask Red.

"Yes, I do it from time to time." Red softly states.

I know Red is waiting on me to start criticizing by the way he answers. Instead, I start asking him questions about how much he makes per delivery, where he must go, and is it easy. I think my questions startle Red because he stumbles a bit over his answers.

After we leave the store, Red tells me he will show me how easy it is to execute the job. We walk down a few more blocks to another corner store in a small shopping complex, which also has a liquor store. In our inner city, liquor stores and corner grocery stores are set up every few blocks. I don't venture into this area much on foot, but I've traveled through here by bike numerous times. This area is part of our neighborhood gang turf, but we are really close to a rival gang's territory about a block away.

Red uses the pay phone while I start talking to some old classmates I haven't seen in about a year. Almost all the guys have already joined the gang in some type of capacity. As I continue talking, I notice a gentleman pulling up in a beat-up old car. Red drifts towards his car in a manner which looks as though he is cutting between cars to get to the store's entryway. I do not notice as Red slips the package Brute gave him to the gentlemen. Red is given another package to give to Brute when Red passes this guy's car. The gentleman gets out of his car heading towards the liquor store. Red comes over to where I am and summons me to leave. While walking home, Red explains the entire transaction.

"Man, how did you make it look so easy and elusive?" I ask Red in amazement.

Red is now moving at more of speedy pace because Brute and Tike are waiting.

"The package I dropped off was the money. The package I am giving Brute is the drugs."

Once we make it back to Brute and Tike, Red slips Brute the drugs. He quickly hands Red two hundred-dollar bills.

"Don't forget I will need you again next week." Brute tells Red.

"You must have forgotten I am going out of town."

"That's right. You make sure you come see me when you get back." Brute replies while giving Red a hug.

"Hey, man. Where are you going?" I ask Red once we make it back to my driveway.

"Homer, I am finally moving back west with my mother." Red tells me with the biggest grin on his face. I am so excited for Red I grab and hug his shoulder.

"I knew you two were butt buddies." Telly suddenly appears and yells out.

It is still kind of early, so we congregate at my house to play some basketball. About twenty minutes later, Grey shows up and we begin to play two-on-two.

Grey is in a sour mood and directs a lot of his frustration towards Telly. With Grey and Telly's past encounters, Telly is normally the instigator. Ten minutes later, Brute and Tike join us to play a game. "Brute, do you have any drugs in your possession?" I ask softly.

"What are you asking, Homer? I do not indulge in the sale of illegal pharmaceuticals." Brute replies sarcastically.

"Red told me everything. Look, Brute, I am not judging you. I cannot let my mother find drugs in her yard."

"I am just giving you a hard time, Homer. I am clean." Brute assures me. Telly knows Red is leaving and wants to take his spot as Brute's runner.

"Brute, please let me know what I need to do to take Red's place." Telly loudly begs Brute as we play around for a moment before starting a game.

"Hey, man, lower your voice." Brute and Tike angrily whisper in unison to Telly because my mother is in plain sight by the patio door.

"Brute, I don't trust him." Tike whispers to Brute.

"Okay, Telly, you will have to prove to me you can handle the job." Brute instructs Telly.

This angers Telly. To show his worthiness, he immediately starts a verbal quarrel with Grey. With Grey already in a bad mood, the verbal quarrel turns into a shoving match.

"Hey, take this to the front yard." I yell knowing my mother is in plain view.

Red stays back because he is growing tired of the violence. I can tell Dirty's death immediately pops into his mind.

"Are you okay?" I ask.

"Man, let them idiots kill each other! However, I don't want to see it!"

I feel the same way, but I cannot let them fight at my house. When I make my way to the front yard, Grey has already pulled out a knife, threatening to cut Telly.

"Grey, what the hell is wrong with you? Put that thing away before someone gets hurt!" I yell to Grey.

Telly sees this as his opportunity to audition for Brute.

Telly rushes Grey, disregarding the small knife in his possession. The force of the fight feels like an offensive tackle against a defensive tackle trying to get to the quarterback. Telly's desire to prove himself to Brute eventually allows him to overpower Grey, removing the knife from his possession. Once Grey is pinned to the ground, Telly takes the altercation a step further by pressing the knife against Grey's throat.

"Am I not the type of guy you want?" Telly yells to Brute with full adrenaline in his voice.

Brute immediately touches Tike so they can leave without responding to Telly. Telly takes his attention away from Grey because he is still begging as he watches them go up the street. This allows Grey to get back on his feet and collect his senses. All Grey needs to do is walk away, but he wants his pride back. Grey then unleashes a series of sucker punches on Telly from behind. I quickly realize why pride is a deadly sin because Telly quickly turns around, knocking Grey back down to the ground with one punch. This punch has some juice behind it because Grey is not a little dude. Grey hits the concrete so hard; he looks as though he bounces off the pavement. Telly sits on top of Grey and begins to choke him by the throat. I see the look in Telly's eyes; he means to kill. Red has made his way up front noticing the same look in Telly's eyes. We both try to pry Telly off Grey. However, Telly's adrenaline has taken over, causing us not to have any success separating the two. Fortunately, Briggs and Hamp have made it to the scene. It takes Hamp, Briggs, and Red to get Telly off Grey. Once they remove Telly, I pin Grey's arms above his head to prevent him from getting up and starting another round. All of this transpires in less than two minutes. Grey is gasping for air while on the ground to get himself together. Briggs asks Grey to leave while they try to calm Telly down. Hamp escorts Grey to the top of the street to ensure he makes his way home without any more fighting.

Slick is beginning to come our way until he sees Hamp coming back down the sidewalk in front of his house. Once I notice Slick, my body shuts down as I almost exorcize my bodily fluids. However, my demons speak to me. They are begging for Slick to come into the driveway. My demons advise I can get a few punches on him as vengeance for what he attempted before someone separates us. Slick must have read my thoughts because he does not venture across the street.

Once things start to calm down, I take off running in the direction of Tike and Brute. I am in such a stride; I dart right past them.

"Hey, Homer! Where the hell are you running to get to?" Brute yells as he summons me to come back.

"I am tired of all the violence, especially after Dirty's death." I state breathlessly, winded from running. I didn't mention the true cause of my anger, which is Slick's attempted rape.

"Man, you need to calm down!" Brute says while Tike agrees with his assessment.

Tike pulls out a brown-looking cigarette.

"Have you ever smoked one of these?" Tike asks.

"No. What is it?"

I know it is weed because I have smelled it when my cousins smoke and from the schoolyard football games. I have been told too many times to say no to drugs. But I am willing to try it to knock the edge off how I am feeling. My demons speak to me to let me know they approve.

When I take the first drag, I do not feel anything but the burn from the smoke in my chest. As we pass it around about three times, I begin to feel the effects. Everything around me starts to slow down. I can focus on really small details like the cracks in the concrete. The birds start to chirp more clearly. I can tell they are singing a song. I notice a bumblebee nestling inside a flower to retrieve its nectar. I am in total astonishment from the effects of this drug. This long one drag begins the sin of gluttony. I take two more hits and thank them for letting me participate.

"Let me know when you need some more. I will proudly hook you up with the good stuff." Tike tells me.

"Homer, are you okay? Make sure you sit outside on the porch before going in the house. Let the effects wear off a bit." Brute advises as I shake my head letting him know I heard him.

While sitting on my back porch for a moment, I slow everything down from this past school year, including Slick's assault. In this moment, I know I could handle just about everything if I feel the way I am feeling from the weed. I sit back in a chair looking up at the sky. I feel like I am in the epicenter of a tornado. Things around me are spiraling out of control while I am sitting back watching all the chaos. Actually, I am the one in the tornado, twisting down a dark road because I cannot handle everything happening to me at this time in my life.

Hole 10 – Revealing the Truth

Once the new school year starts, I am struggling to keep my sanity. I am lashing out more at school. I really do not care that my grades are suffering. I only give enough effort to get passing grades. The only place I feel secure is on the golf course. This is where I put all my energy. The walk home from school is rooted in my mind daily. I am unsure if Slick is waiting by the woods for a sneak attack. I begin carrying a homemade knife I conceal under my sleeve to slightly injure an attacker to get away to safety.

One snowy day, school is let out early before the road conditions worsen causing the city buses to stop running for the day. When I walk down the steep front steps of the school, I notice Slick's car parked by the bus stop. My mother asks him to pick us up so my sister and I will not have to deal with the winter weather from the bus trip home. I immediately duck back into the school, retreating to my locker to think of a way to avoid the ride home. I ask my sister's friend to relay a message to Elise that I have already taken the bus home. Ms. Loper overhears me telling my lie because the halls are almost empty. The acoustics of my conversation drifts into her classroom.

"Homer, please step into my office ASAP." Ms. Loper orders me as she leans into the hallway. I do not say anything, and head immediately into her classroom.

"I want you to be honest with me and tell me what is going on with you. Your teachers have been telling me you are not giving your all. I notice you have been aloof, and you also do not smile like you used to when I first met you. Now, tell me before I request a session with the school counselor." she expresses sternly.

The smiling part is easy because I have braces.

"I am embarrassed by my braces, ma'am." I respond quickly.

"You don't have to smile to do your classwork. Is anyone bothering you at school?"

For a moment, I think about telling her everything.

"Can you promise me what I tell you will stay between us? I don't want this reported or leaked to anyone, especially to my mother." I ask Ms. Loper softly.

I figure I can end this today and begin to move forward to get back to normal. However, my demons emerge, instructing me to hold this episode inside for a little while longer. Once Ms. Loper closes the door, I follow my demons' instructions.

"I need to get to the bus stop before they stop running."

I do not give her a chance to stop me.

"Homer! Homer! Get back here right now."

She keeps calling me back, but I ignore her as I cut into a side hallway leading to an exit I can slip out of unnoticed. The demons tell me I am doing the right thing by not confessing because Ms. Loper will have to report the incident. If confronted, the demons warn me it is Slick's word against mine.

I manage to go unnoticed as I board the bus at a stop before the one in front of my school. When we reach the stop in front of the school, I notice Slick has pulled away. Some of my sister's classmates are on the bus. I sit and chat with them before I get to my transfer stop. I am relieved to hear Elise left with another girl whose mom is going to drop her off a little later in the evening.

Upon arriving at my transfer stop, the weather is getting worse. I do not mind the rain and snow mixture, but the wind is painful. I can tolerate this little bit of torture to avoid Slick. While in deep thought to get my mind off the cold, I notice a familiar-looking vehicle pulling up next to the bus stop. It is Grey's dad, offering me a ride home. I am about to decline until the heat slapping me in my face from the window being down makes the offer too hard to resist. I haven't heard or even thought about Grey since the fight between him and Telly.

"How is Grey doing? I haven't seen much of him since the spring."

"Grey is doing well in school. He played football for the middle school team during the fall. Have you heard from Red?" Grey's father asks.

"I haven't heard from him since he left to go back west with his mother."

We have a long conversation about a few topics on the way home, our rate of speed is reduced because of the wintry precipitation. I am glad Grey has finally turned his negative energy into something positive. I don't think Grey told his dad about his near-death experience with Telly.

My mother is already home when Grey's dad drops me off. I thank him for giving me a ride and for the conversation. Our conversation allowed me to take my mind off my worries for a moment.

"Why didn't you ride home with Slick? Damn it, Homer, you can catch a cold in this weather." my mother asks.

"I didn't see him because I went out a side exit to avoid the dismissal chaos at school." I say, lying to Mother.

A few days later, Silver and I are at the corner store playing some video games to pass the time before a school basketball game. I break away for a moment to get some change for the machine. One of our classmates asks me to buy him something since I am heading towards the cashier. While acknowledging him, I accidentally bump into a guy named Fred who is traveling in the opposite direction down the same aisle. Fred is in my sister's class but is a lot older due to being retained a few times for poor grades. He is a lot bigger than I with an intimidating presence. Fred is part of the local guys who are assigned to my middle school because they live in the housing projects within walking distance. Fred and his crew hang out in front of the store daily to give everyone the notification this is their spot. They give the kids who are in the honors program a hard time. They feel we are weak because we focus on our academics. Fred is upset because I step on his new sneakers. Stepping on brand new sneakers is a cardinal sin.

"Hey, man! My fault." I immediately apologize.

"Watch where you're going, Preppie!" Fred tells me angrily.

"It was an accident." I reply, smirking.

"You think this is funny white boy?"

"No, I am just saying my bad." I reply with a grin.

I am not afraid of this guy because I have been around guys like this in my neighborhood at home. As long as they are talking and do not feel like getting physical, everything is good. I learn during my fights in my neighborhood to watch for the little things to see if a guy will really come after you. You study if the neck begins to flair a bit or by the vein on the forehead. If the vein is visible, the percentage is high you are about to brawl. The biggest factor is true gangsters do not talk before swinging. They act first and talk later. I do not notice either sign, so I go back to the real business of getting change for the video game machine.

As Silver and I prepare to leave the store to attend the game, Fred knocks on the window to summon me to come out to the parking lot. I do not pay him any mind because the situation is not serious to me. When I walk in front of his crew to go across the street to the gym, I hear a few of the guys mumble they will get me after the game. Something instantly triggers in my mind. I can use bullying as a way to hide the real reason I am struggling. If Ms. Loper, the school counselor, or my mother want a reason, I can use this approach.

During the game, I go into deep thought about how to play this angle. By the middle of the fourth period, I completely forget these guys threating me before the game. I do not have a game plan just in case these guys decide to jump me in the parking lot. I suddenly remember I have my homemade knife in my backpack. I casually slip it under my sleeve while making my way to my mom's car.

During the next few weeks, these guys try to intimidate me to the best of their ability. I am using being bullied more and more to hide the root cause of my difficulties. My mother finally gets wind of my plan and asks the school counselor to intervene.

When the counselor questions me about my grades and the individuals he thinks are bothering me, I remain silent. I do not give any information or names. I am shocked when Fred arrives in his office a few moments later. The counselor tells us he has been monitoring our interactions. He warns Fred he is already close to being expelled for other reasons. During his lecture, my mind wonders off about the day of the assault. I am having vivid visions as I begin to sweat profusely.

"Homer, are you okay?" The counselor asks.

"It is too hot in this office. There is no air circulation."

"Boy, the window is open. It is about forty degrees outside. I know you can feel the air flowing from across the room."

I am having a panic attack. Fred gives me a look confirming I am some sort of freak.

"Fred. Help Homer into the hallway. I am going to get him a cold towel."

"Hey, white boy, are you okay?" Fred asks in a whisper.

He can't ask me out loud because it goes against his gangster demeanor. I can tell he is genuinely concerned as I tell him no. The secretary phones my mother's office and hands me the phone. My mother wants to know if I need to go to the ER or the doctor. I tell her the doctor is fine.

While sitting on the bench in the school's office waiting on my mother to pick me up, I do not know who I am anymore. I am letting Slick ruin my life. I am purposely messing up in school so my mother will put me on punishment because of my grades. The only course I am excelling in is algebra. The only reason I keep this grade high is because I know my mother will ask Slick to tutor me to get my grade back up to par. If I am on punishment, I cannot go outside. If I am not outside, I can avoid Slick.

The downside is my golf game is suffering tremendously. I am sneaking into the backyard in the evenings to smoke weed to ease my anxiety and to get some sleep. I am turning down advances from girls in my class because I feel this bastard has taken my ability to show anyone any form of affection. I think about coming clean in the middle of the school hallway, but the embarrassment and shame is too immense to expose my feelings.

My mother is so confused, trying to figure out what is wrong with me she calls my father to try to intervene. He chooses MLK weekend to pick me up and take me to see some of my grandfather's relatives in southern Mississippi. On the ride down, we really don't say much to each other. I take a long nap because I feel comfortable riding in the car knowing am I moving far away from my troubles. I am fending for a hit of weed, but my father's cigarette smoke is filling in the void.

My dad wants to see some of his cousins who live in the remote rural areas of the county as soon as we arrive. I can tell my dad feels comfortable in this type of setting. My father is a smart man who has worked in city government all his life. I think the stress and bureaucracy in politics weighs on him at times and the country life is a great escape. I feel the tranquility of the rural surrounding. As I stretch from the ride down, I stop to look around for a few minutes.

I have been to the country many times, but this is the first time I just sort of look around to admire the scenery. I am used to seeing miles and miles of concrete, buildings, and houses. It is breathtaking to look over the horizon and wonder where it will end. Instead of hearing cars, police, fire sirens, and airplanes, I am listening to the birds and the wind blowing through the trees. The weather is nice for January, which only intensifies the experience. I record this scenery in my mind.

My dad spots one of his cousins working on something in a field about five hundred yards from where we are parked. He quickly has us jump back into his SUV, puts it in 4X4 mode, and takes off on the terrain in the direction of the work. We arrive on the scene just in time to assist his cousin with trying to remove a tree stump from the ground. The method to retrieve the stump isn't working as he planned. Just like Superman in a phone booth, my father swoops to the back of his truck, quickly puts on his work overalls, and springs into action. The hook drilled into the stump isn't deep enough to support the wrench attached to the tractor trying to extract the stump. Our cousin states there is a bigger hook in the barn on the other side of the house from the direction we just came. My dad goes to the back of the truck and grabs two beers from his cooler and turns to me to go get the hooks. I turn to start walking when he tells me to take his truck. I am baffled and ask him to repeat himself. He repeats to take the truck as he takes the top off his beer bottle. Plus, he states my little brother needs to go to the bathroom. I am only used to driving his tractor when he cuts grass at my great aunt's house. He reassures me driving his truck is the same as driving the tractor. I do what he requests and drive up to the house so my brother can use the bathroom and retrieve the hooks from the barn.

I don't press the gas too much; I just steer the SUV as I let the car move by being in drive. I let my brother out and then drive to the barn to retrieve the hooks. I am not sure what size to take so I grab all the ones I think are needed. I turn around, get my brother, and proceed to return to where my father and cousin are waiting.

By the time we return, they are opening their second beer.

"Did you get the hook?"

"I wasn't sure on the right size, so I grabbed a few different sizes."

"He is smarter than you give him credit." Our cousin states.

I quickly figure out I am being tested by my father. I am not sure why he is testing me, but I pass.

"Homer. I notice you were taking it easy on the terrain." my cousin adds.

"I was afraid if I went faster, I may have lost control of the vehicle."

"You learned this while driving the tractor, right? I told you the tractor was a good starting point." my father states as he sorts through the hooks so he and our cousin can finish the job.

I am given the keys and told to drive the country highway. We are off to the house where my grandmother was raised. Outside of a tractor, this is my first driving experience. My father isn't telling me if I am doing good or bad, so I take it I am doing pretty good. I don't go over 35 miles per hour. It's no big deal because it doesn't seem we are in a big hurry.

My grandmother's brothers and sisters always keep the house in great shape even though the structure is over a hundred years old. My great aunt greets us as we get out of the car and asks if we are hungry. I am starving so I follow her to the kitchen. Besides playing golf, eating is my favorite past time.

"Did you come down to help on the expansion of the house?" my aunt asks.

"I am not sure." I respond while I am demolishing a plate of food.

As soon as I take the last bite, she quickly replenishes my plate. My father walks in and she fixes him a plate while they exchange pleasantries about what was going on in our hometown.

"You need to put some more food on your plate. This is good eating." "This is his second plate." my aunt quickly intervenes.

By the time he gets over how big my appetite has grown, I am asking for another piece of cornbread.

"Has everyone eaten yet?" my father asks my aunt.

"Don't worry about that. There is plenty." My aunt responds while cutting me a huge piece of pound cake.

"When was the last time you had something to eat, Homer?" my father asks.

"Leave Homer alone, he is a growing boy. Remember how you used to eat when you were his age." My grandmother states as she enters the kitchen. I almost choke when she walks in. I wasn't expecting to see her. I attempt to get up and give her a hug, but she quickly presses my shoulder down and kisses my forehead. She pours me a huge glass of her special sweet tea to help me wash down my food.

After eating, I go out back where some of my great uncles and cousins are congregating, going over the building plans for the annexation. As the assignments are given, I am on wheelbarrow duty. Over the next few hours, we work tirelessly, leveling the land. I never knew I had muscles in certain areas of my body. The wheelbarrow feels like it is triple my body weight, but I manage to get all the loads to the designated area. We get most of the work done until a thunderstorm moves in rapidly, disrupting our completion. I am upset because I don't want to come back tomorrow to do this work again.

I stay at my cousin Mickey's house in town; he is about a year older than I, while my father stays with his cousin who lives a few houses down. They normally stay up drinking and telling stories to the wee hours of the morning. Because of the rain, they start drinking a little earlier. We find out rain is forecasted for the entire weekend, so my hard labor is over.

I haven't seen Mickey in a while. He is impressed with how much I have grown. Between the summer and throughout the school year, I have grown about six inches. I am still skinny as a rail and starting to look older than my age. We are almost the same height, but way off regarding physical dexterity.

It is still early in the evening, so I ride with him to hang out with some of his friends. We end up at the local gym to play basketball and goof off for a while. I am asked to play because they are one short. Even though I am physically exhausted from moving dirt all day and already had a shower, I join in the game. My competitive side, who has been hiding for a while, surfaces just as it did when I agreed to compete in the schoolyard football games. I don't want these guys to think I can't play, or I am afraid because of my appearance.

As we begin to play, I can tell these guys are intermediate players. My cousin, who is a pretty good athlete, is the best player on the opposing team. I ask to switch to him on defense because his game reminds me of Red's. Once I get a steal off him as he tries to go back door on a pick and roll, I try my best to get everyone on my team involved with the offense. My arms are tired so I know my jump shot will be off a bit. I take advantage of driving the lane to pass to a team member whose defender switches off to guard me the closer I get to the basket. Even though I am making spectacular passes, these guys are missing wide open routine baskets. If I was at home, I would easily have given my teammates a tongue lashing. However, I don't know these guys, so I decide to leave it alone.

During a break, some of my cousin's friends are giving him a hard time about my style of playing basketball. They tease Mickey about me having more essence in my game. For a moment, I feel they will tease him about having a white cousin. Even though my cousin and I share the same last name, we are quite different in appearance. You can tell he is more African American than I, even though we share some physical features. As we depart, his friends shake my hand and ask me to help Mickey find his inner pepper. They are teasing him because he acts white but looks black.

When we make it back to his house, his older sister is there with some of her friends. They have just returned from a school function and are planning a sleepover since the weather forecast is projecting thunderstorms for the rest of the evening. I notice they are all gorgeous and some swift fantasies run through my head, but the dreams are quickly washed away when my stomach starts to growl. I know they are having a feast where my father is staying, so Mickey and I get cleaned up and head up the street to eat.

While leaving Mickey's house to go eat, one of the girls and I make eye contact. I can tell there is an attraction between us, but I play it off and stroll along up the street.

Just as I imagine, they are having an extensive meal. I can't believe I am looking at all this food. I give a few hugs to family members I have not seen in a while and quickly make my way to the table. Between Mickey and me, I think we sit for about ninety minutes, eating as much as possible. My aunts and cousins are happy with the amount of food we consume. They feel our appetite is a complement for the hard work put into preparing the meal. My father is embarrassed by my appetite, but I keep being told to help myself because there is plenty.

"Homer, are you staying at our house?" Mickey's mother asks.

"It seems a sleepover is happening. I was going to try the couch, but I don't think there is any room."

"You and your brother use the twin beds in Mickey's room and Mickey can use our bed. We will stay in the guest house outback with your father." She directs.

Damn, I must be in paradise. I have a full stomach and now I am about to sleep in a house with beautiful girls.

After dessert and some small talk with family about how golf is going, I am getting tired and want to go to sleep so Mickey and I head back to his house. It is a slow process because I am literally dragging my little brother due to him already being half sleep. Once we get in the house, I place him in my cousin's bed and jump in the other bed to get some rest. I am taking a power nap when my cousin storms in to tell me the girl I made eye contact with is asking him a lot of questions about me.

"You need to make your way to the den and start mingling before you waste a big opportunity."

"She has to be close to seventeen and I am only fourteen."

"Homer, you look just as old as I do. You must not pay attention to yourself in the mirror." Mickey expresses while laughing.

He is right. I am ashamed of the person I look at every day.

"Homer, go in the den, be yourself, and everything will turn out okay. This young lady is feeling you." Mickey adds.

I get up and make my way to the bathroom to make sure I am presentable and do the breath and under arm check. Then off to the den I go.

Mickey's sister quickly approaches me to tell me the same thing Mickey has already emphasized. I explain to her about the age gap, but she tells me to not concern myself about the age difference. I smell food, so I make my way to the kitchen to figure out the aroma. It is pizza from a national chain I do not care for all too well. They do have some sweets and I grab some to munch on. MTV is on the television while everyone is having their own conversations on different subjects.

During all the laughing and some outbursts, I hear a voice from behind telling me hello. I know who it is and sort of hesitate before I respond. I turn around to respond to her greeting. She introduces herself as Ola and chuckles a bit when I tell her my name is Homer. We talk between the entryway from the kitchen and the den. The entryway is wide, so we don't have any issues with the traffic going in and out of the kitchen. However, the noise makes it a bit hard to hear. I suggest we go outside so we can communicate a little better.

The conversation is good because we are totally different people. We ask each other numerous questions because our backgrounds are so diverse. I am intrigued by Ola because she never brings up my appearance. Questions surface about our love lives and Ola reveals to me she is dealing with a bad breakup. She notes her ex may show up just to give her a hard time. I explain my love life is quite simple because I don't have one.

Suddenly, I begin to fill a chill in the air as a storm is brewing. Loud thunder starts to clap, awakening my little brother from his sleep. He is afraid due to being in a house with strange people. He knows my older cousins but wants some insurance someone he is comfortable with is nearby. He makes his way outside to where Ola and I are sitting. I insist we need to make our way inside because of the oncoming rain and the sudden drop in temperature. Ola sweetly asks me if I need help putting him back to sleep and I graciously accept the assistance.

My little brother gets a little conceited due to receiving a lot of attention from the girls in the house. I take him to make his way back to the bed. Ola is pulled away for a moment for some girl talk. They are getting ready to watch some horror movies on videotape. My brother begs me to let him stay up to watch and runs into the kitchen to get him something to snack on. I think this is cool because the first hint of fear from the movie will probably send him running to the back within twenty minutes. I have seen this movie and can't torture myself to sit through viewing it again, so I make my way to the back to rest up for a moment.

I snuggled in and started reading one of Mickey's wrestling magazines before I try to go back to check on my brother, who I hope will be running down the hallway to hide in the bed soon. I doze off for a moment, but I hear my dad in the front room questioning if I am sleep. He comes back to the room and asks me if I am good.

"I figured your brother was up because he doesn't like thunderstorms. I will take him back up the street with me."

My brother hears this and tries to negotiate staying here but loses the argument.

"There are some nice-looking girls up front. Why are you back here?" my dad whispers.

"One of them already has their eye on him." Mickey interjects while entering his room to grab a comforter from the top of his closet.

"I guess he is alright after all." My dad adds. "No need to worry about getting up early tomorrow. We will probably leave sometime in the afternoon." I am relieved so I roll over to call it a night.

I am abruptly awakened by the thunder that feels as though it is right above the house. I am so startled I can't force myself back to sleep. I am in Mickey's room alone with a small lamp providing some reading light resting on the nightstand between both beds. I am thirsty so I head up front to get something to drink and I notice I am not the only one who was tired. Only a couple of my cousin's friends are still awake, and the rest have fallen asleep on the den floor or in her room. As I make my way back to bed, I notice Mickey is draped across his parent's bed snoring. As I snuggle in again,

I am stunned when the lamp suddenly turns off while I am facing the wall lying in bed.

"Can I nestle next to you? The storm is a bit frightening?" Ola asks.

I do not say yes or no. I just let her climb into the bed. We softly continue our conversation from outside.

Ola's complexion is dark. She is a lot shorter than I, but her body is fully developed. Ola senses I am a bit nervous and asks me to loosen up a bit. I really don't know what to do. So, I do what I think is right and begin kissing her neck. She responds well so I move to her ear, causing Ola to begin giggling a bit.

"This is something new for me. You may have to show me what to do." I state shyly as I move back to kissing her neck.

"You are doing fine." Ola softly states as she lines my face up with her lips to begin kissing me.

While we kiss, my mind is in a confused state. However, my body loves every moment of the experience. Thoughts are racing through my mind that this is my time. I will finally have a sexual experience. As Ola turns me on my back, I think about having to find some protection and hoping my inexperience will not cause her any displeasure. I attempt to ease all tension by telling myself I want to do this with Ola. I think back to my grandfather's advice on waiting for the perfect one who will let me pollinate her flower. At this moment, I know Ola is the one.

As Ola straddles me, she grabs my hands and lets me caress her breasts. I don't care for the feeling because her shirt is a barrier between my hands and her skin. I move my hands to her stomach area and slowly place my hands under her shirt and back up to her breast. Ola grabs my hands to show me how she likes to be touched. I must have done something right because Ola begins to avidly kiss and touch me all over. As she makes her way to different areas of my body, my vision starts to get cloudy, and I begin to feel uncomfortable. Ola continues to passionately kiss me. She starts moving her hand slowly down to my private area. I am erect and firm as I can be, but I still have an uneasy feeling. When Ola puts her hands in my shorts, I freeze and jolt her hand away.

In a short moment of time, I relive the encounter with Slick all over again. The current situation is far from his assault, but the scar of the occasion is still fresh, and it hurts. I quickly excuse myself and rush to the bathroom. As I run water over my face, I begin to look at myself in the mirror. This is when I realize Slick is ruining me from personal enjoyment and growth. I cannot let this go on any further. I am letting this incident wreck my life. I am not functioning at school, my passion for golf is fading, and I feel I am becoming a social misfit. My demons' surface to inform me I have a beautiful young lady ready to make love to me in the other room and I am letting Slick ruin it from two hundred and fifty miles away. As I dry my face and hands, I make a vow to the demons and myself to not let this incident control my life any longer.

While walking back to the bedroom, I feel embarrassed. I am delighted to see Ola has not left.

"I need to apologize."

"I need to apologize to you, Homer. I feel like I am using you right now to get over the hurt from my boyfriend." Ola interrupts and expresses.

"I need to get something off my chest." I express to Ola as I explain in a long affirmation about what Slick tried to do and how it is affecting me.

"This is why I pushed you away." I state softly and begin to immediately feel a tremendous weight slowly lifting itself off my body.

My mind starts to feel relaxed and clear without the help of some weed.

"The reason my boyfriend and I are having problems is due to not having sex with him." Ola expresses.

I immediately find this odd because I am under the impression we were about to have sex.

"What were we about to do?" I ask.

"Touching, kissing, and rubbing are my definition of sex. I am not ready for full intercourse."

"I am not ready myself. Is this what you do with your boyfriend? And what makes me so different that you would give into to me so easily?" I ask while laughing.

Ola explains her boyfriend stopped engaging in conversations like we had earlier.

"All I want is someone to talk and feel connected with and you made me feel connected to you. When you kissed my neck, I thought it was genuine and passionate. When you told me you were in newfound territory, I was more drawn to you. I feel what we were doing was right and I will not apologize for letting my feelings loose. Therefore, I broke up with him because I couldn't let my feelings flow freely, and you were making me feel special by taking your time. If it is okay with you, I would like it if you came back into the bed and continue from where we left off."

"Where we left off to a certain point?" I reply jokingly. "You do know I am only fourteen."

"You do not carry yourself like one, plus it doesn't matter because I just turned sixteen."

When I get back in the bed, we talk and laugh a little while longer. The storm sounds like it is getting more intense, forcing us to become quiet as the lightning starts illuminating the room. Ola gets closer and begins to kiss me again. Things get intense and passionate again. As we go further along, I feel like a shell is being removed from my body and mind. It is like a caterpillar turning into a butterfly. We remove each other's shirts and I grow even firmer by noticing her bare breasts from the lightning outside. We tell each other where to touch to satisfy our desires. After all the intense touching, rubbing, and kissing, we please each other without having sexual intercourse. Due to me being tired from earlier in the day, it doesn't take me long to fall asleep.

We all wake up late the next day. Ola and I catch a lot of teasing from her friends. We both play innocent as though nothing happened. My cousin grills me to tell him the details, but I let him know we just talked most of the night until we fell asleep. My cousin's dad calls the house to let everyone know they are making breakfast at the house up the street. I don't need to be swayed so I put on my shoes and make my way to eat. I eat like I missed all my meals the previous day. After making a vow to myself and the experience a few hours earlier, I feel like a new person. Once again, a couple of relatives tease my dad, wondering if he feeds me at home. My dad again states he is a little embarrassed by my appetite, but he quickly receives ridicule from the family about his eating habits at my age.

After eating, my dad states we will leave shortly because we couldn't do much work because of last night's rain. I leave to go back to my cousin's house to get cleaned up and ready to go. As we approach the house, I see Ola talking to one of guys we played basketball with yesterday and assume this is her ex-boyfriend. He greets us and I walk past her like we don't know each other. After their conversation, Ola approaches me in the back to explain what was going on. I tell her I understand, and she doesn't owe me an explanation.

"Did you work everything out?" I ask.

"Not really. He was sort of begging."

"Let it go and move on to someone who can make you happy." I express with concern.

"One of the girls must have tipped him off to what happened last night. This is the only reason he would show up unannounced so early." Ola explains.

We talk about me leaving shortly and how we both enjoyed last night. We both know we cannot carry on a long-distance relationship.

"Homer, you will find someone special real soon and she will be very lucky. If there is truth to divine intervention and we meet up again later down the line where the moon and stars align together, I will jump at the chance to be that special someone." Ola states before we give each other one final kiss.

After this precious moment is over, it quickly fades as we go our separate directions.

I don't say much on the ride home. I sit in back and think about the weekend's events. My grandmother rides back to Memphis with us. My father bringing her home was one of the intentions of the trip.

"What's going on in that head of yours, Homer?" she asks softly, just under the music playing where only we can hear each other.

I open up to her and explain everything from this weekend expecting to get fussed at a bit, but I trust this lady candidly.

"As odd as this may sound, this is God speaking to you. The young lady is right. You are special, Homer. Once you realize this, the world will open more to give you different perspectives and allow you to move to the next level in God's plan. Now, I expect to see you at church for a while so you can repent for your foolishness this weekend." she expresses while giving me a firm grip of my hand.

"Yes, ma'am!" I reply with a grin.

When I return to school on Tuesday, I tell Ms. Loper I need to talk to her at some point during the day. She lets me know to come by during lunch. Unlike all the other times in the past, I am not hesitant expressing my feelings.

"Promise me whatever we discuss stays in this room. I will deny everything if you report what we discuss with anyone."

"You have my word, Homer."

I finally come clean to an adult as to why I am acting in such a manner. I explain lying about being bullied to cover up the truth. I admit to her the vow I took to not let it consume me anymore. Ms. Loper just sits on her desk, clutching the edge in anger.

"At some point, you will have to confront Slick." Ms. Loper suggests.

"I agree, but it has to be on my terms." I express with confidence.

Ms. Loper is quiet as she jumps from her desk to give me a hug.

"I am so proud of you for finally getting this off your chest. I know this has not been easy. You have true courage Homer."

When I leave her room, I feel the burden easing from my body while my mind is becoming so much clearer.

Hole 11 – Eruption

After my conversation with Ms. Loper, things at school go back to normal as I am able to focus more intensely on my schoolwork. The rest of the eighth and ninth grade school year go by in a blur. My friendship with Gold and Silver is growing stronger. My golf and baseball skills are developing at a high level along with my physical statue. Silver and I begin to meet up on Saturdays at the mall to waste the afternoon goofing off and chasing girls. Gold, Silver, and I have a few classes together during the ninth grade, which causes us to grow closer as we sometimes chat and laugh during down time in class.

I only have one incident at school. A kid in the seventh grade tries to show his toughness by sucker punching me after a football game. This kid hits me and runs off into the crowd. Once again, the school officer intervenes before I can retaliate. I catch a little teasing about it, but most people feel as though he is a coward for not sticking around after the punch. I meet with the principal about the incident. This instance is not a big deal to me, but she still makes me identify the kid from our school ID database. I play dumb until she threatens to suspend me for not cooperating. Once we are together in the principal's office, the kid comes clean as to why he punched me.

"I hit him because of the way he looks. He thinks his white skin gives him an advantage against all of us. He walks around with too much confidence and like nothing will bother him." He states as I almost jump out of my seat in anger.

I am infuriated because I feel like I will never gain acceptance from my own people because of my fair complexion. The darker kids in elementary and middle school think I receive special treatment due to me having a lighter skin tone. The Caucasian kids I deal with in baseball and golf do not accept me because they sense I am not one of them. I am growing frustrated because looking this way is a curse. I feel I cannot categorize myself with any nationality. In a moment of anger, I unleash a verbal tirade on this kid.

"How would you feel if I hit you because you are black?" I ask.

He cannot respond to the question. I notice a look of satisfaction from my principal as I lecture him on the stupidity of his reasoning.

"I am proud of the way you expressed yourself. I can tell you are maturing." My principal states after our meeting.

One of the happiest days of my youth is the last day of the ninth grade. I want to put this place behind me and move on to high school. However, I will never forget Ms. Loper. She was my homeroom teacher for three years and my literature teacher in the ninth grade. Since we are considered high school freshmen, we are taking exams on the final day of school. After my last exam, I make my way to see Ms. Loper one last time.

When I enter her room, she is packing up in a hurry to begin her summer vacation.

"Why are you still here? I figured you would have been on the first bus home." Ms. Loper asks.

"I had to come by and thank you for everything you have done for me over the past three years. I know I was a pain sometimes. I wanted to let you know I will never forget you!" I express before I start to tear up as I give her a hug.

"I will miss you, too! You were one of my special challenges over the course of three years. Just remember what we talked about and continue to be the best Homer you can be. Don't ever forget to stay true to yourself and everything else will come easy. You will only know how extraordinary you are when you realize you are special. I know you are headed for great things Homer."

I do not get the gist of what she is saying until years later. I never find out what happened to Ms. Loper because I never return to my middle school after this day. I never heard if she retired or passed away. Whether Ms. Loper is in her physical or spiritual being, she is one of those special teachers who never gets the praise or the glory for their work. From the bottom of my heart, I thank you for helping me get out of one of the worst funks of my life.

Unfortunately, this is not the lasting memory I have of this place. While cleaning out my locker, I am jumped from behind by three kids while I am slumped over clearing out everything. I am hit in the head by the metal door which makes my vision fuzzy. These guys do a number on me until I manage to stun one of the assailants with a punch to the throat and an elbow to another guy's temple. The building is clear except for the maintenance engineer checking all floors. He manages to scare them off.

"We finally got his white ass!" One of the attacker's states as they run down the opposite side of the hallway through a rear exit.

By some miracle, I am not bruised or scarred. No one is around to witness the episode, so I don't have to deal with any ridicule. The maintenance engineer checks me to see if I am okay and lets me go about my business. I am not sure who these guys are but apparently, they have been waiting for this moment for a while.

Our summer trip to my grandparent's is short due to my mother setting up my sister and I to volunteer at a summer camp, playing in a few golf tournaments, and my baseball season. I realize working with small kids is fun. In some twisted way, I feel I can protect them from predators like Slick while they are in my presence.

At the camp, an incident occurs, sparking a lot of anger inside of me. I am walking the smaller kids to the swimming pool about six hundred yards away from the day camp's facility. Three guys are hanging out by some huge trees along our pathway to the pool. I do not pay them any attention because I am too busy making sure my age group does not lag while talking and playing. One of my six-year-olds makes his way to the back of the line so I can tie his shoes.

"Why are you helping this little nigger?" One of the guys by the tree asks in an aggressive tone.

When I turn to address the question, I notice these guys have the persona of Skinheads. They dress like them with the haircuts and boots. They must feel I am disrespecting the Caucasian race because they see me as a white guy helping a little black kid. Through their eyes, I am violating their beliefs or code of conduct.

"Hey guys, I am trying to help a six-year-old kid get to the pool so he can have some fun in this heat." I express to the three gentlemen.

"Boy, didn't you hear what we told to you?" Another one of the three asks.

"Hey, kid, go ahead and catch up to the rest of the group. I will be there shortly." I whisper calmly to the little boy after tying his shoes.

As soon as the kid begins to run off, he is tripped by one of the guys in the group. The fall causes him to scrape his knee and elbow. I rush over to the child because he is crying.

"Hey, be a big boy for me. Run and alert the head counselor and Ms. Elise." I whisper to the little boy.

Once he is out of the way of danger, I immediately confront the guy who tripped him.

"Why did you trip him and who in the hell are you talking to?" I respond curiously.

All three guys approach me to give me a sales pitch about the Skinhead organization. I abruptly cut them off because I need to catch up with my group.

"Remember, fellow brother, we do not help niggers." The leader reiterates.

I should just walk off, but my demons surface letting me know it is time to unleash some of my anger. Because of my true ethnic background, I cannot let this slide. My maternal grandmother gave me the background on the origin of the word. It always makes me sick to hear the word used in anger, such as this case. She explained to me this word is the most offensive word in the English language. Its origins stem from the Colonial Era. Over time, it derived into a classification of slaves in America. The derivative became mostly used by the white man to label and categorize all people of dark complexion in the beginning of the 1900s.

"You realize you are using the word incorrectly. The word is meant for the unsophisticated and unintelligent." I define to the three as their eyes light up like they are gaining a recruit to join the cause.

They pause for a moment to hear what I am about to elucidate.

"You are the ones who are acting like niggers because why would a grown man want to push down a six-year-old kid. Why don't you try knocking me down like that?" I aggressively yell to the group.

They begin to surround me. I am not afraid because my adrenaline is pumping at a high rate. In an instant, I think about all the things bothering me as I clench my fist. As the so-call leader says something derogatory, I launch into him with all the pain, emotion, hurt, and rage I coil into my fists. I know I cannot take on all three guys, but I am going to do some damage to this idiot. My punches are not having an effect because he dodges my first blow while quickly going into a fetal position on the ground. Even in this position, I am laying everything I have into whatever is exposed. I know I am hurting this kid because I have his blood on my knuckles and my fists are hurting. While I punch and kick this guy, his two friends are beating the hell out of me from the back.

The little kid alerts the head counselor and my sister. By the time they both look back, I am in a heavy-duty brawl with these assholes. They quickly sprint to my aid, but I am about two hundred yards away. I am in the zone, trying to punish the guy I am hitting. This place of gratification and focus causes me not to feel the kicks and punches the other two guys are landing. I let everything bottled up inside just rush out of me in a rage. I am crying as I pulverize this guy because I am feeling relief from this stress with each punch I land. The head counselor finally arrives as the two guys who are taking target practice on me quickly scatter. He has to forcefully pull me off the guy I am assaulting. He struggles with me until he has to take the drastic measure of slamming me down on the hot pavement. The adrenaline is still pumping because I still want to get up and go after the guy. Elise applies a firm bear hug on me to prevent me from going after those guys again.

I am fired from my volunteer role because the director feels like I am too volatile. She feels I may possibly erupt at the wrong moment and inadvertently hurt one of the kids. It pains me I will not be around some of the kids I have developed a relationship with. On the flip side, it feels so good letting the stress out of my system. When I leave to go home, all the kids in my age group hug me. The little kid who was tripped tells his parents about the incident. They make a pitch to the director that I was defending a child. Even though the director takes their suggestion seriously, I am told not to return. The young man's father thanks me for standing up for his son.

After the adrenaline wears off, I begin to feel the effects of the beating I endured. My pants are ripped, my back is bruised, my hands are swollen, and my neck is hurting from being slammed to the concrete. It takes a few days to recover. I need the recovery because the floodgates are about to open.

When I get home, I am immediately put on punishment after being let go from my volunteer job. I see Red who has returned for the summer to stay with his grandmother. My mother knows it has been about two years since we last saw each other. She gives me a reprieve to stay out on the front porch so we can catch up. Both Red and I have experienced a growth spurt since he left. I've grown about eight inches, but my weight has not caught up with my height. Red has shot up about six inches. He looks as though his weight is proportioned with his height. Red is fussing because I am taller than him. He cannot stand I have hit the six-foot mark in height before him. We are both going on fifteen and starting to have facial hair emerge.

"What happened to you, Homer?"

"I got into a fight today at work."

"I see you haven't changed a bit. Where is Telly?" Red replies, laughing after telling him the story.

"Well, Telly filled in for you as Brute's runner. However, something happened on a delivery causing Telly to have to leave the house behind mine to go stay with other relatives. Brute was looking for him because a high dollar shipment came up missing. According to Brute, he had to pay for the merchandise out of his pocket. Telly stopped by my house one day after school. He did not tell me where he was staying, but he was bragging about how much money he was making a day. I could tell by the way he was dressed he was getting heavy in the drug game. It seemed like he went from rags to riches overnight. When I ran into Brute a few weeks later, I put two and two together to equate Telly stole the merchandise to start his own business."

The outcome of this incident is unknown because this the last day I see Telly. I am not sure what happened to him over time. No one really brought his name up again.

Of course, Red wants to know what Brute's crew is up to in the neighborhood.

"Brute has expanded his operation and territory. Tike oversees the gang and Brute is in full control of the drugs. They bought a house around the block they use as a hangout. They have homes in the suburbs, apartments to stash merchandise, and numerous cars they change out like the sneakers every week." I tell Red.

"Damn, Homer, how do you know all this information?"

"I buy weed from them on occasion. They are generous with the bags I purchase. If I buy a twenty-dollar bag, they give me forty dollars' worth of weed."

"Mister 'I am on track with my life' is smoking weed? I am shocked. Where do you keep it?"

"Come on, I will show you my hiding place."

We go around back so I can show him my hiding spot. I show him the brick I removed from a wall dividing our patio from an elevated flowerbed. Red is impressed with the way I wrapped the weed and papers so they will not get wet. The loose brick is unnoticeable unless you are going to remove all of them to rebuild the wall. He wants to smoke some right now, but we must wait until my mother is not home.

The next day, I am awakened by the doorbell a little after eleven. Even though I am grounded, I stay home while my mother is at work. I always enjoy being at home. This punishment is like a vacation because it too hot outside to do anything except to stay in the house. I know it is Red before I open the door. I let him in and head downstairs to get something to eat.

"Tell me about how things are back west," I ask Red.

Red does not hesitate to give full details. While I am eating, I listen to him tell me about his school, his house, and his lies about girls.

"Are you still a virgin, Homer?"

"Yes!" I answer immediately. "I have kissed some girls, but sex is far from my mind."

I am talking to girls over the phone and meeting them when Silver and I get together at the mall on some Saturdays. However, I am not close to anything physical like my experience with Ola. This does not mean I am not noticing girls. Trust me, I am paying close attention. I still run into Free on occasions when she is at her aunt's house. We talk or whatever, but we are not at the point like we were in the sixth grade.

Red is describing his sex life like he is a porn star. I think he knows I can tell he is lying, but the stories are entertaining. He is trying to coerce me into getting Free and her cousin to come down to the house, but I am not taking the bait. Red makes fun of my virginity to try to get me to give into peer pressure. I am holding close to my grandfather's advice on sex.

"I want to have a beautiful experience and not just a feeling."

"You will probably go crazy by the time you have sex." Red states while laughing at me.

I do not pay him any attention because I know it will happen eventually.

Finally, my punishment is lifted for good behavior. I make sure the house is clean every day and the yard is cut when needed. I can get back out in the world.

Tee is starting to host basketball games in his backyard. Tee's yard is wide open giving us plenty of room to play ball. Tee's stepfather watches us play to keep everybody in line. Tee's stepfather is cool. He has a heavy influence on me with some of the talks we have between games. He sits back with his quarts of beer and gives us his opinions with pure honesty. I always enjoy the folks who are honest even if I do not like what they are saying. The games in Tee's backyard are extremely physical. This style of play often leads to some shoving matches. Red and I play peacemakers because I do not want the games to return to my backyard.

Red is becoming a more dominant player. He is getting harder to defend. Red makes his high school team as a freshman. I am feeling good for Red. He has come a long way since Dirty's death. I am hoping he stays grounded on his current path. The games are eventually halted from Tee's house because too many people are showing up, causing Tee's stepfather to shut it down.

One afternoon, Grey shows up to my house at Red's request. We make our way to the backyard to play some ball. Red wants to smoke a bit before we start, so I roll up some weed and take a few hits with Grey and Red. Tee and Que show up, but I will not let them back until I store away my weed. We do not have enough to play teams until Slick and Hamp walk into the backyard. I am in shock, but the buzz from the weed is helping me to quickly recover. After my confession with Ms. Loper, I told myself I will eventually confront Slick. It seems God is listening to me because I have been praying to completely get over what he tried to do to me.

Once we pick teams, I end up on the same team as Slick. I quickly protest and switch up with Red. Red, Slick, and Que will take on Grey, Tee, and I. Everyone is in shock because I give Red's team a clear advantage. I give Red's team an even better advantage when I tell Grey I will guard Slick instead of Red. Red is jumping up and down because he knows his team will win four out of seven easily. I do not care about winning today because this is personal.

As soon as the game starts, I immediately get physical with Slick. I am pushing him, elbowing, scratching, and taking cheap shots to the body whenever I get the opportunity. Even though Slick is the nerdy type, he is a pretty good player and no pushover.

"Why are you being so aggressive Homer?" Slick asks angrily while stopping the game.

"You know what this is about." I yell to Slick as everyone around us is perplexed by my actions. The first game takes forever. Every time Slick gets the ball, I am fouling the hell out of him.

"Homer, calm down a bit so we can play at a better pace. You are tripping out." Red suggests while taking a water break after the first game.

"Fuck you! This is between Slick and I. It's personal!" I angrily reply to Red.

When the second game starts, Slick decides he will get physical with me in return for the way I treated him in the first game. I am getting him more upset because I am not calling fouls.

"I know you love touching me. Are you getting turned on?" I whisper to Slick while dribbling the basketball to setup a play.

I can tell he is furious.

"Do you want to touch me like you did that afternoon?" I ask Slick while guarding him on defense.

After this question, he reaches his boiling point.

"Do you want me to tell your mother about you smoking weed in the backyard?" Slick yells.

"Do you want me to give her the full details on what you tried to do me?" I reply.

Once again, everyone is looking on in confusion. Hamp intervenes by asking Grey to switch to defend Slick because he knows we are about to come to blows.

When play resumes, Que sets a pick on Grey, forcing me to defend Slick. As Slick dribbles past me to attempt a layup, I intentionally slam my forearm into his neck forcing him backwards onto the concrete. Everyone rushes over to see if Slick is okay while he is on the pavement. While Slick is lying on the concrete, vivid details of his assault replay in my head. In those few short moments, I relive the entire event over in my mind. I infuse all the suffering, hurt, and disappointment over the last three years into my fists. My demons surface to tell me this is my chance. As soon as Slick gets to his feet, I take all my anger out with one punch to the right temple and a clean shot to his left jaw. Grey and Hamp immediately jump over to restrain me while Slick lays on the ground gasping for air. I do not care if he dies while lying on the pavement. I want to get on with my life. I desperately want him to suffer like I did for almost three years.

Hamp tries to rough me up a bit for striking his friend, but Red and Grey immediately bring it to a halt. Grey is still upset by the punch he received when we were in the third grade. Grey tells Hamp to back off. Hamp does not pursue the issue further because he realizes he will have his hands full with Grey because he has grown taller and bigger at the age of fifteen compared to his size at eight years old. Hamp then decides to focus his attention on Slick.

"Is this over? Is everything resolved between us?" Slick asks once he emerges from the pavement.

"Yes!" I reply with a tear in my eye.

With all the lawsuits today on sexual assaults, I wonder what may have occurred if I took Ms. Loper's advice and reported the incident. I realize I could have killed Slick with the punch to the throat. Since I did not report the sexual assault, I easily could have been charged with premeditated murder. My life would have been over. I immediately realized why wrath is considered a deadly sin. It takes over your actions causing you to lose control. However, I feel vindicated when it surfaces. Slick tried to molest Boom, Red and Que. He did it the same way by gaining our parents trust and luring us into his web over time. Once I explain my actions to the group, they all give me props for doing what they feel should have been done a long time ago.

Slick is punished for his attempts on us. Though it is not a prison sentence, God carries out his reprimand. Slick never marries and stays with his parents. Slick obtains numerous degrees in various studies but turns down jobs with lucrative salaries without giving a good quality reason. Recently, I saw Slick getting his mail while dropping my kids off at my mother's house. Slick looks old and run down even though we are about ten years apart in age. The memory of what he did surfaces for a moment then dissipates as I think about my retaliation on the basketball court. I forgave Slick a long time ago. I truly let the issue go on the court. This may sound hypocritical, but I am glad the Lord allowed me to lash out at Slick in the way I did. I believe if I kept letting this fester beyond this day, I would have resorted to falling deeper into the sin of gluttony by further chemically resolving the problem. God lifts this burden because he has a blessing ready for me to accept very soon.

I am starting High School in a few days. I am glad to have this finally behind me. I never see Hamp again after this incident. Hamp's name is like Telly's. No one ever mentions him; so, we forget about his existence.

After unleashing my wrath on Slick, I shower and go to Tee's house to play video games and to calm down a bit. Tee tells his stepfather what happened in my backyard. His stepfather decides to talk to me for a moment to see if I okay from a mental aspect.

"Sir, I had to resolve this the way I did. The reason for the altercation was plaguing my judgment. It was, in a sense, controlling me. I do not like feeling I am not in control." I express while intentionally trying not to give too many details.

"Sometimes in life you must pick your battles. In this case, you chose to end the situation the best way you needed to feel closure. Based on what you and Tee have explained to me, I think you handled yourself well."

He is right. For the first time in three years, I feel free and alive again. Relieving this burden makes me feel as though I am floating while walking.

After a couple of hours, I leave Tee's house because a storm is brewing. While walking home, lightning is getting close as the rain starts to fall. I look up to the sky for a split second to witness a grey cloud explode with the crackle of thunder and the beauty of lightning. My soul is taken on a journey through the clouds into the heart of the storm. While I am standing in the epicenter, everything around me is being washed away while I am floating in the most peaceful spot. A voice emerges telling me I am ready for the next phase in my life and something beautiful is about to enter my world. As soon as the voice stops, I am taken back through the clouds. I am banged around in the clouds and washed by rain until my soul reenters my body. I can see my physical shell at a standstill waiting for my soul to reenter. Upon entry, my body picks up right where it left off heading towards my home to avoid the storm. On this night, I sleep soundly, waking up with a renewed mind anticipating the next beautiful phase the voice references.

Hole 12 – Forever Changed

I am excited about starting high school. I know Gold, Silver, and a few others from my middle school will also be attending Central. My sister and I are back under the same roof.

The first day is typical. We have to find our way around this goliath of a building. My homeroom is on the top floor on the far side of the building. The building is not fully air-conditioned causing the heat to rise to the floor where my homeroom is located. The population of the school is massive. About two thousand kids from the tenth to the twelfth grade are funneling through the hallways every hour. I am on edge based on past experiences. However, the individuals I meet across campus are cool people. I think it is unique we take classes with juniors and seniors. The upperclassmen I come across are not snobbish or classify us in an appalling manner because we are fresh meat on the scene. Most of them know me because of my sister, so I am fitting in with all grade levels.

I run into Gold while passing classes. We both whisper to each other about all the beautiful girls we have come across throughout the course of the day. The best-looking ones are in our sophomore class. We bump into Silver going the other direction. Silver is already in pimp mode talking to a girl he just met. We find out we all have the same lunch period. We promise to discuss our findings during this time.

Because the school is partially air-conditioned, we are dismissed at noon because of the heat. We all congregate in the lobby area of the school to give a recap of our day and get an overall view of the females we will see daily. Members of the high school fraternities are trying to get some of us to listen to their sales pitch about joining. I know this is trouble because I witnessed some of the initiations behind my elementary school for these so-called social clubs. In my opinion, they are gangs hiding behind unaffiliated Greek letters. Due to the way the gang affiliations are structured in my neighborhood, I will stay neutral.

I cannot leave immediately after school because my mother wants me to talk to the golf and baseball coach about joining the team. I have some time to mingle for a moment. We do not talk to Silver much because he is talking to every girl catching his eye. Gold and I are talking to folks we just met and introducing ourselves to people we do not know. Gold wants me to walk with him towards the front of the school on his way to the bus stop. I walk with Gold halfway down the steps to the main entrance. I explain to him why I must head back inside. I am called by my sister to get a few details on how long my meetings will last. My sister does not care how long it will take because she wants to socialize. Some seniors, who I know from middle school, begin to joke with me about staying out of trouble with the girls. I notice a group of girls heading my way as I am about to enter the building. It is a no brainer; I will hold the door open for them. I am still joking with the seniors as I turn to open the door for the young ladies. While executing my act of chivalry, my life changes forever.

I see a young lady who is my definition of perfection. She's wearing a green multicolored sundress, which matches her eyes perfectly. Her hair is pulled back from her face exposing her beige buttercream skin. She is a lot shorter than myself but is the perfect height in my eyes. As she passes through the entryway, she smiles at me. I am blown away by her smile because she also has braces. Her scent takes my breath away. I am in love before she says hello. I hold the door open as the entire group walks through, but I only notice her. I watch as she walks down the steps a bit where the seniors I just talked with flock to the group. I watch her for a little while longer while she talks to the group of guys because I am mesmerized. I quickly dismiss her from my mind because she is out of my league. I hastily get back to my agenda of meeting with the coaches. However, I must get another glimpse before I head upstairs. She knows I am watching because she gives me a little wave. Regardless of the fact I think she is out of my league; cupid has hit me with his arrow.

Later in the afternoon, I call Gold to tell him about this girl. Gold puts Silver on three-way calling to talk about his findings for the day. We talk for about an hour, discussing everything about school except for classes. It is still early when we get off the phone. I stay in my room to watch a little television because it is scorching hot outside. A couple of hours later, the phone rings. I figure the phone is for my sister, so I do not waste the effort by answering the phone.

"Homer, a girl name Nadera is on the phone." My mother yells from her bedroom.

I am curious so I pick up the phone in my room to talk to this mystery girl. The voice is perfect pitch. It isn't too high or too low.

"Do you know whom you are speaking with?" the sweet voice asks.

I am a little puzzled. I haven't given anyone my phone number.

"My name is Nadera. You held the door open for me and my friends this afternoon."

I almost fall out of my bed when I discover it is her. Silver gave her my number. Nadera and Silver are cousins. I guess Silver feels I am respectable enough to date a member of his family. I do not care how the conversation occurred for her to request my number. Silver tells me years later it was a coin flip decision to bring Nadera and myself together. He explains it was between me and another gentleman we both are acquaintances with at middle school. Whatever tactic or strategy gave me the advantage for Silver to bring us together, I am eternally grateful. All I ever needed before this moment was a small opening to get through something. Nadera calling was the opening I need to spark a conversation.

The dialogue is fantastic. Even though we only talk for about twenty minutes, it seems we discuss everything under the sun. The more Nadera talks, the more my heart is slowly transferring over to her. I make sure I get her number before I get off the phone. We agree to meet up at some point during school the next day. As soon as I hang up the phone, I immediately roll backwards in excitement. I fall off the bed, hitting the floor with a thud.

The next day at school is like the first day. We are on an abbreviated schedule due to the heat. We are dismissed early, and everyone congregates to the lobby area.

I am hanging with Gold and a few other friends when Nadera and her group walk to where we are assembled. As soon as she begins to talk, everything around me shuts down. Even though the lobby has over a thousand people socializing, I drown all the activity out to focus on Nadera. We talk for a while when she realizes she left something in her locker. I walk with her as we talk more and more to get to know each other better. The side of building where Nadera's locker is located feels like your grandmother's kitchen while frying chicken. Her locker is on the basement floor of the school. The distance and the heat are worth it to be in Nadera's company. I have been around other girls up to this point, but I never felt like this around one. Even though I am nervous, my words and actions are effortlessness and flawless. I can tell Nadera is falling for me just as I am for her.

After we leave her locker, I walk her to where her father will pick her up to go home. He is running a bit late. His tardiness is prescribed at the right time. I miss a free ride home, but it is worth it. When Nadera's father arrives, we promise to call each other at some point in the evening. We both know it will be later than sooner because the academic standards of our high school are extremely high, requiring intense studying. Although it is the second day of school, we have a lot of work to get done.

Once the heat dissipates, we are back on a full schedule at school. Nadera and I do not have any classes together and have different lunch schedules. I make an effort to see her before we go to homeroom. We both try to see as much of each other as we can after school. Coordinating time is hard because Nadera is a Junior Varsity cheerleader, and I am on the golf and baseball team. With her homeroom being on the basement floor and mine being on the fourth floor, I am running the massive steps at the school every day to make sure I do not get caught by the tardy bell.

One day after school, all activities are canceled due to an emergency staff meeting. I have plenty of time to kill. I am hoping Nadera has not left for the day. I am relieved she is still on campus after rushing to her locker. I haven't seen her at all today. The wait turns out to be a blessing because she is looking extremely radiant. She is wearing a black dress suit with red trim. Her hair is down. The little bit of makeup Nadera is wearing makes her face look like perfection.

"My mother is running late. Do you mind waiting with me until she arrives?" Nadera asks. Are you kidding me?

Nadera could ask me to run behind the car to her house and I would agree.

We wait by a side staircase located by a small entry way into the school, which leads to the administration offices. It appears we spend hours on the steps, laughing and talking. It has been a few weeks since we met but we do not consider ourselves an item. While conversing on the steps, we solidify our feelings and officially become a couple. We definitely make it official because we both lean over and kiss each other. Even though I have kissed other girls before Nadera, this kiss is the one. The kisses from the past cannot measure in rank. This kiss makes the ground shake, I hear fireworks in the background, and my whole body feels like it has been lifted off the ground. Her lips are soft, and her tongue movement is flawless. Once we finish, I cannot do anything but smile. Her mother arrives soon after. Before Nadera heads to the car, she takes a step back to give me a quick kiss goodbye.

I am on a cloud for the rest of the afternoon while playing basketball with the guys at Tee's house. My game is at an all-time best because I am riding the feeling of falling in love. Once I am settled in for the evening and prepare for the next day, I make sure I call Nadera once my sister jumps in the shower. I am tired so I make the conversation short.

"Guess what, Homer!" Nadera states while we are about to hang up.

"What?" I reply.

"I love you!"

"I love you too, Nadera," I reply without hesitation. "One day, I am going to marry you."

"What are you talking about, boy? You must be tired."

"Okay, Nadera, just wait and see."

I have fallen in love a couple of times since Nadera, but no one has made me feel the way she made me feel when someone says those three words.

We have a day off from school for a teacher in service meeting. Due to making the golf team, we must put in a certain amount of practice away from school. I am returning from playing a practice round with my uncle when Grey drives by in his dad's truck. He just received his learner's permit but really shouldn't be on the road just yet. Grey is about image. He feels everyone seeing him driving in the neighborhood is a plus for his reputation. While Grey is parking in the driveway, I hear the phone ring from the front porch. My sister tells me Silver is on the phone. Silver is at Nadera's house. After some small talk, he inquires if Grey can swing by and pick him up to take him to his aunt's house who lives across from the elementary school up the street from me. Grey is down for the trip. After we get the directions, he feels comfortable the distance to Nadera's house is not too far. I beg Grey to give me about ten minutes because I need to wash the smell of the golf course off me if I am to see Nadera.

I remember the feeling of anticipation and keenness of seeing her once we turn on Nadera's street. Silver meets us in the driveway. I am not entering the house without having a formal invitation. We talk for a moment before Nadera comes out of the house. Nadera greets me with a solid hug and a kiss on the cheek. My heart is softening as she hugs me. Her touch sets off things inside of me no one has made me experience. She invites me inside to meet her older sister and younger brother. Her parents are not home. Nadera's older sister is trying to feel me out a bit to make sure I am a good fit for her younger sister. Her sister and I talk for about twenty minutes. I can tell Nadera is getting a little tired of the questioning because she wants us to have a few minutes of alone time. Silver is scrambling around the house, making sure he gathers all his belongings. Nadera pulls me to the living room area while her brother goes back outside. Her sister goes upstairs to take a phone call.

Once we are alone, Nadera passionately lines my lips up with hers and kisses me like I have never been kissed. Everything is in order. Our breath is fresh, we both have confidence kissing each other, and our heads are at the perfect angle, even though I am eight inches taller than Nadera. My hormones go fanatical when she kisses around my neck. I slowly move my hands to her lower back to pull her closer to me. I am amazed by the softness of her body. Since we have never discussed sex, I am not going to push Nadera into anything to make her feel uncomfortable. I am in love with Nadera, so I will let her lead.

"We need to stop because Grey needs to get back home."

"Yes, maybe we should stop." Nadera states while still kissing me.

We make a pitiful attempt at stopping. We cannot halt kissing each other. In the background we hear Silver and Nadera's younger brother fussing about Silver promising to walk him to the store. Grey interjects, offering to drive Silver around the corner. Nadera and I laugh because we have gained about fifteen more minutes together. I sit down for a brief pause in one of the living room chairs. I am fully engaged at this moment, and I know she can feel me. Nadera begins to kiss me again. I know it is time to stop because I want more than just kissing. I explain to Nadera how I am feeling. We mutually agree this is not the right time and setting. When I get up from the chair, the fervent kissing of each other has weakened my legs. We make it back to the den area just as Silver and Grey return from the store. Grey is ready to depart. Silver does another last-minute sweep to make sure he is not leaving anything behind. I sit on the couch for a moment to calm my feelings down a bit. Nadera sits next to me and softly holds my hand for the little time

143

we have left. Grey and Silver exit the house first. Nadera leans over to give me another adoring kiss before I leave. She deliberately kisses me in a way to leave me infatuated until our next encounter. While walking out the door, Nadera looks me square in my eyes and softly tells me how much she loves me. As we pull off from her house, I know I am love struck.

I am invited back a few days later to meet Nadera's parents. I am fortunate enough to get my aunt to drop me off. I am a little nervous, but the tension is lifted when my aunt and Nadera's mom know each other from high school. They grew up a few streets over from each other in their old Orange Mound neighborhood. Nadera's mom graduated high school a year before my father. Her mother pulls her yearbook from 1961 to show me pictures of my father. I admit the evening is pleasant.

Nadera and I sit in the living room watching videos for a couple of hours. We talk about the ups and downs of school. We are enjoying the moment because our time at school is limited to a few minutes in the morning and literally a few seconds after school. I occasionally slip out of class during her lunch period. I only stay a few moments before anyone notices I am somewhere I do not belong. We kiss and cuddle a bit, but nothing on the scale of my first visit. We indirectly talk about physical intimacy. Nadera touches on her virginity, which sparks a discussion on religion. I do not have a problem with any of her morals. I know this girl is the one. I can wait as long as possible because I am in love with every fiber of her being. Both of us are not ready for this stage in our lives but we are curious.

I wish I can say things remain smooth, but our relationship begins to fall apart. Between extracurricular activities, inquisitiveness, and schoolwork, we barely have time for each other. As a cheerleader, Nadera is being approached by guys sparking her curiosity. By having a pretty good sophomore season on the golf team which is covered by the media and preparing for spring baseball, I am being approached by different girls who also spark my interest. In high school, dating and relationships are a game. You learn how to win by losing.

I will never forget the day Nadera calls me to break off our relationship.

"We just cannot find the time to see each other. It seems you are not putting forth an effort to make it work." Nadera informs me over the phone.

"Nadera, I promise to commit more of myself to you because fall is almost over. My extracurricular activities are minimal during the winter months. Just hold on a little while longer. I really do love you. I do not want our relationship to end like this." I state, pleading.

In the end, Nadera rejects my plea, and we mutually agree to part ways.

At first, I am not upset because I figure I can get my point across face to face at a party we are attending later in the evening. I ride to the party with Gold and Bronze because the event is close to my house. To my surprise, Nadera does not acknowledge my presence. She ignores me, acting as though we never existed as a couple.

"What's with Nadera? Is everything good between you two?" Gold asks.

"We broke up this afternoon. I am not sure why she is not talking to me."

I am standing outside for a moment to catch the late October breeze. When I return to the main party area, I suddenly hear a loud commotion. Nadera is on the couch, kissing another guy in front of everyone. This action is like a stab to my heart. I am not upset about her kissing someone else. I am hurt because she is not honest enough to tell me outright about meeting someone else during our earlier discussion.

Since my mother is out of town, I am to go over my dad's house after the party. However, I have Bronze drop me off at home so I can get my thoughts together after what transpired. I call my dad to pick me up, but he decides to let me stay where I am until the next morning because it is late.

While alone in the house, the quietness causes the heartbreak to settle inside me. I begin to cry. I start thinking about where and when things went wrong. I immediately go to my stash and roll up a nice size blunt to completely liberate how I am feeling. The last time I touched my stash was the day I fought Slick. After I met Nadera, I didn't need to smoke because I was flying high on love. The weed has lost its potency from being stashed away so long. I throw it out behind a tree in the backyard.

While walking around the house, I stumble across my mother's liquor collection along with all her vinyl albums. I promised myself I would never drink anymore after I got totally wasted at my cousin's wedding about a year ago. However, I need something to take the edge off. I pour some bourbon over ice and start looking through my mother's album collection. I've heard her playing some of the albums on Saturday mornings. However, I never really paid attention to the melody or the lyrics. I put on an *Isley Brothers* album out of curiosity and begin drinking my bourbon while still researching her library of music. The music is more of a high than the alcohol. It seems as though the Isley Brothers, O'Jays, and Marvin Gaye are singing about my specific situation. I go to the front porch to listen and drink to forget the events of the day.

The phone rings at about two in the morning. I figure it is my father checking up on me, but it is Nadera's friend,

Aimee. Aimee knows I am hurting and wants to make sure I am okay. I take the phone to the front porch to begin telling her how I am feeling. After I cry to her, she gives me more details about the guy Nadera was kissing. I really didn't care about this fool because he is just a flavor of the month guy.

"Aimee, I put everything I had into this relationship. The reason I am hurting is because I feel Nadera lied about how she truly felt about us."

"Homer, I understand why you are upset. However, there is something you need to realize. You have been so wrapped up in Nadera; I do not think you know other girls are interested in you. Trust me; you will not be lonely for too long." Aimee confesses.

Her disclosure breaks me out of my funk instantly. I want to know which girls are interested, but I refrain from asking the question. Aimee is being a good friend because she talks to me until I am ready to fall asleep. We talk about everything except for Nadera. Aimee and I stay close throughout high school. We can open our hearts to each other about our dating lives, problems at home, and our schoolwork.

In a short period of time, I was flying high on love to have it come crashing down in an instance. Nadera got me good. I am not able to eat or sleep for a few days because of my broken heart. My mother has to feed me on occasions because I am too hurt to eat. During this time, I vow to never again expose myself to another girl because I never want to feel like this again. I never lose my love for Nadera. We still call each other from time to time to make sure we are doing okay. My heart always sinks when I am in her presence. Her voice absolutely makes me melt when we talk. My hardened feelings prevent me from having meaningful relationships with other girls. I will always keep a soft spot for Nadera. Her name defines her perfectly: a rarity.

Hole 13 – Moving On

I am struggling to get back to normal. Nadera and I are still friends. We exchange Christmas gifts and I send her flowers on Valentine's Day. I spend most of my sophomore year in high school getting over her. Right before winter turns to spring, I realize it is time for me to move on. My friendship with Gold, Silver, and Bronze is still strong, but my relationships in the neighborhood are plummeting. I spend a lot of time at Tee's house, but I do not play basketball or hang out like I have done in the past. Because of school, I do not have time for anything. I am playing golf and baseball at a high level. All my spare time is consumed with practicing both sports.

I find a way to suppress my feelings for Nadera by dating girls from all over the city. Me, Silver, Gold, Bronze, and a few other guys at our school are going to or crashing parties all over town. The girls I am meeting are just substitutes to keep my mind off my heartache. Things start off well, but I dump them as soon as I develop feelings or things go sour. Gold is the only one who can see through my charade. He knows I only care for one person. By using the girls as fill-ins, I become sexually active for all the wrong reasons. My curiosity finally turns into reality, but I am not gaining any feeling from the experiences. The girls are the overly aggressive ones my grandfather warned me about. However, I am listening to my demons. In my defense, fifteen-year-old hormones are hard to dampen once ignited.

My body is starting to fill in with my height. I am still skinny, but my muscle dexterity is starting to surface due to weight training from my high school baseball coach. Age is not a factor because I am sexually active with older women. I am not talking about juniors and seniors in high school. Both women are in their mid-thirties. My mother would kill one of her closest friends if she finds out this lady is sexing me crazy. She introduces me to some different pleasures, and it blows my mind. This lady is good to me. She helps me get over my heartache. She is at a crossroad in her life after a terrible relationship. We both use each other as temporary voids until the next person surfaces. We continue our on and off physical relationship until the summer before my senior year in high school. I cannot reveal the identity of this woman because I promise to keep it a secret. In today's world, they would charge this woman with statutory rape. Rape is such a harsh word. It does not describe our relationship; it was consensual.

My cousins teach me sex and relationships are two different things. Sex is just a feeling or a past time. On the other hand, relationships are an emotional connection and a close association between a man and a woman. This lady and I have an emotional connection.

My cousin marries her childhood sweetheart. He is very influential in my overall growth into becoming a man, as well as my sexual growth. Brick teaches me about condoms, as well as how to treat a lady, and how to piece a woman together to make a man happy. Brick is the man. He has the house, car, clothes, and it is all legitimate. Brick receives full benefits and disability due to a freak accident on a military training mission. The military pays him a nice settlement once they realize his injuries will never heal correctly. You will never know Brick is in ill health due to his physical stature.

149

Brick becomes my golf partner after he learns the game after catching the golf bug during a vacation. Being on the course with Brick and my uncle is always refreshing because I can talk to them about anything.

"Brick, do you remember the first time you were heartbroken?" I ask while teeing off on a hole.

I confess to him about how I treat girls because I am still in love with Nadera. I explain what happened at the party the night we ended our relationship.

"Homer, don't put anything past these women! They can be more scandalous and treacherous than a man! If you think she is not doing anything against you, she probably is." Brick states with passion. This advice serves me well throughout my life.

"A girl broke my heart so bad, I eventually had to write her off completely." Brick confesses while walking from the clubhouse to the car.

"What happened to the girl?"

"I married her." Brick replies while chuckling. "Homer, keep doing what you are doing to find out what you like and dislike in regard to women."

"Why I am I not gaining anything from my sexual experiences?"

"If you feel good afterwards, then you are getting something from it. Keep doing what you are doing because you will eventually find the feeling you are looking for. Just make sure you keep using those condoms."

This is why I love Brick. He keeps it really simple. He never tells me what I want to hear. He tells me what I need to hear.

I throw all my energy into school, work, and sports. During the spring months of the school year, I am playing and practicing baseball five days a week. I am practicing golf seven days a week. It sounds like a lot, but my activities are keeping me out of trouble. Most of the guys I know with too much idle time are getting caught up in negativity. My only downfall is my sin of gluttony. I am drinking a lot of alcohol and smoking a lot of weed. I drink a lot of beer because I love the taste. Buying alcohol is easy in the neighborhood. If you give the clerk an extra few dollars, they will let you slide with a school ID. A quart of beer, which normally costs two dollars, will cost about five unless you get one of the neighborhood drunks to buy it for you. The catch is you must buy the drunk the drink of his choice.

On my way home from practices, I will get a quart of beer, drink it before I get home, and occasionally smoke a blunt while walking. The high I achieve helps me to manage everything going on in my life. Even though I am going at breakneck speed, the weed slows everything down.

Once I get home, I eat, do my homework, and possibly talk to a few girls on the phone before going to sleep. I am not getting much rest until the weekend. On Saturdays, I sleep until the afternoon hours. On Sundays, I am up playing golf with my uncle at the crack of dawn. Once finished, I come back home and go back to sleep.

One weekend, my family members from Mississippi are in town for a funeral. My cousin Mickey has his driver's license so my dad lets him use his car so we can ride around for a while. I try to get Silver to meet us at the mall, but he does not have a ride. He asks if we can pick him up from Nadera's house, but I initially refuse. I do not want to see her because I know my feelings will surface again. I am at the point where I feel I am getting over our relationship. Silver cons me into picking him up by letting me know Nadera is not at home. I should have gone with my first instinct because, as usual, Silver is not ready when we arrive.

151

After about fifteen minutes, Nadera pulls up while we are waiting in the driveway. I am a little buzzed from lack of sleep and a few beers I stole from my dad's house. Mickey spots Nadera and immediately wants to know more about her. Mickey is a good-looking kid who fits her appearance prerequisite. After exchanging pleasantries with her mother, I introduce Mickey to Nadera. While my cousin lays his game on her, I wait to see if Nadera will tell him about us because I want to know if she still cares about me.

She doesn't say anything while soaking up the attention she is receiving from him. The feelings that surface so quickly are immediately dissolved. As they converse, I go to the car and wait for Silver so we can leave.

"Hey man, is she with someone? I would love to get to know her a little better." Mickey asks as we pull off from the house.

"She is off limits. I made the mistake of hooking Nadera up with Homer." Silver responds.

"Damn Homer, why didn't you tell me about your relationship? I would have backed off."

"I just realized I am over it." I reply in a whisper.

We finally arrive at the mall. Mickey and Silver are the center of attention. They are in full pimp mode, getting phone numbers from every girl willing to give them a little attention. Because Mickey is only in town for the weekend, he is looking for a quick score. Due to Mickey's looks, there are plenty of girls at the mall willing to give him what he wants. I am not in the mood to put my full energy into gathering a stack of phone numbers. I am enjoying sitting back watching all the women walking around the mall. I still do this today as a married man. I will watch a crowd of women as a spectator sport. I have been all over the U.S, Europe, Asia, Mexico, and

Canada but Memphis ranks in the top three of having the most beautiful women.

My mindset is somewhere else because I have a junior golf tournament in a few days. Plus, I am emotionally upset by seeing Nadera. I bump into a girl I am courting named Leslie and her friends from a rival high school. Leslie and I talk on the phone sometimes, but I do not put in a bold effort to pursue her full time. I tell Mickey and Silver I will catch up with them shortly at the ice-skating rink, which is the centerpiece of the mall. Due to being upset about Nadera, I am listening to Leslie talk but I am not hearing a word she is saying. Her words are sounding like the adult voices from the *Charlie Brown* cartoons.

When we arrive at one of the anchor stores in the mall, the girls in the group notice some guys from their school gathered in front of the entryway. Leslie and I are about a few paces behind the group. As we get closer, one of the guys looks familiar. I cannot put a name to his face. Leslie and I continue talking as I stop my progress and lean on one of the clear guard rails to look at the floor below. I notice the group of guys looking at me awkwardly. The high school they attend is a rival because they have similar academic standards as our school. The only difference is the school is in a high-class area of town. I am not worried about the evil looks or stares because this type of stuff does not bother me anymore. If one of them wants to scrap, I know it will not be much of a challenge. My mentality is to back away from any altercation because I do not want to jeopardize participating in my golf tournaments or my summer league baseball schedule.

While leaning over to see the activity going on downstairs, I notice Silver and Mickey coming up the escalator. Once they reach the second floor, Silver goes over to greet two guys in the group. I turn my head in the other direction to see Brute and Tike with a couple of girls. They have their normal entourage not too far behind them because this is how dope boys travel. Brute comes over and quickly strikes up a conversation. I whisper to Leslie to go ahead with her friends, and I will catch up with her shortly after I chat with Brute. Brute is laughing at me because he has never seen me talking to a girl. He yells over to Tike saying, "Look who is trying to get some game."

"Where have been you hiding and how are things progressing?" Brute asks with sincerity.

"I am focusing on school and my sports."

"You still playing the white man's game, Homer?" Brute teases. "Do you have the right gear for baseball and golf?"

"My mother got me everything I need for the summer. I have a tournament in Dallas next weekend. I have everything I need."

Brute reaches in his pocket to give me five brand new one-hundred-dollar bills.

"Homer, you are representing the neighborhood. Since you are representing Alcy, you are representing me. I have to make sure you have the best of everything."

I know this is drug money, but Brute will consider it an insult if I turn the money down. Brute has been good to me over the years. He has diverted a lot of negativities away from others in my neighborhood who wished me harm. I do not believe Brute's kindness has an ulterior motive. Brute has never asked for anything in return, except for me to follow the path I am on to reach my goals.

"Are there any strings attached? Like I said, I have everything I need." I ask Brute.

"If you were a girl, then strings would be attached." Brute replies, laughing. "Look, Homer, I have more money than I can spend. Take the money as a gift."

Mickey looks on in shock as I take the money and put it in my pocket. I notice Free is in the group with Tike and Brute. She comes over and gives me the biggest hug while kissing me on the cheek. Free is looking fantastic. I haven't seen her in a while. Free is out with her brother, who is part of Brute's entourage. Silver notices Free as well. He comes up to greet her and to talk for a moment.

"Who are those guys you are talking to Silver?" Free asks.

"I do not know all of them. One of them dated my cousin." Silver responds.

Damn, this is why the guy's face looks familiar. He is the guy Nadera kissed at the party. This also explains the evil look he is giving me.

"Homer, you know Leslie is his ex-girlfriend." Silver whispers to inform me.

Once Silver reveals this information, I begin to laugh. Karma is a bitch. While he was getting with Nadera, I was getting with his girlfriend. I met Leslie at about the same time my relationship ended with Nadera.

The group of guys and girls start to make their way to the food court. Leslie makes her way between Brute's entourage to ask me to join her. She also informs me one of the girls in her group is interested in Mickey. She then gives me a kiss on the cheek in front of Free. Leslie is not trying to be discrete when she gives me the kiss. Leslie's ex-boyfriend sees everything. I can tell he is visibly upset. The guys bump fists with Silver as they depart. Leslie's ex-boyfriend intentionally makes his way close to me.

"That's why I stole your bitch you white bastard." He whispers, referring to Nadera.

Brute overhears his comment.

"Do you know this fool, Homer?" Brute asks.

I already know what this means. Brute is ready to fire into this guy. I must quickly defuse the situation because Brute's crew will stomp the crap out of this dude. Plus, I know these guys are strapped. I explain the history to Brute about the situation. He laughs when I inform him Leslie is the guy's ex-girlfriend. I exchange handshakes and hugs with Brute and Tike before heading to the food court. Whew! Crisis avoided.

"Remember, Homer! As long as I am around, no one will fuck with you." Brute reminds me before he departs.

I nod, letting him know I appreciate it as we engage in another farewell hug.

We make our way to the food court to meet up with the girls. I tell Mickey about the girl who is interested in him. He quizzes me during the walk, but I do not have much information because I do not know which girl Leslie is referencing. Once we make our way to the line they are standing in, Leslie introduces Mickey to the girl. She is fine but having beautiful women wanting to meet Mickey is nothing new to him. He is used to having nice looking women throwing themselves at his mercy.

I am not hungry, but Leslie buys me a strawberry milkshake. I softly thank her because it is a nice gesture. Mickey whispers to me he can tell Leslie really likes me and I should give her a chance. His advice marinates in my head for a moment. I really haven't given anyone a chance since my relationship with Nadera. Aimee told me I need to move on during a phone conversation a few weeks ago. Leslie is smart and attractive, but I cannot see this clearly because my heart is still broken.

Leslie asks if we can come by her friend's house because they are doing a mini sleepover. Mickey has a hormone rush and instantly asks for directions. We agree to meet about eleven. It is only about eight o'clock. I want to drop Silver off as soon as possible to get over the emotional trauma of seeing Nadera twice in one day. Leslie kisses me on the cheek again, gives me a hug, and whispers she is anticipating seeing me later.

I sit in the back seat during the ride to Nadera's house while Silver and Mickey talk about the women they encountered in the mall. Neither Mickey nor I say anything about going to Leslie's friend's house.

"Homer, I see you and Leslie got along very well. Why weren't you talking to any other girls?" Silver asks.

"Shoot, I am thinking about this golf tournament next week."

"Why did you take the money from that guy, Homer?" Mickey asks.

"It's complicated to explain if you are not from my neighborhood." I reply as Mickey starts giving me a lecture.

I shrug his advice off and take a quick nap since we have a nice ride before we get to Nadera's house. Once we arrive, Nadera's mother asks me to come in for a moment. At first, I tell her we have to go, but my cousin turns off the car because he wants to see Nadera again. Her parents inquire about my family. I have a brief conversation with her father about golf before her brother pulls me away to the living room to show me a new video game. This is exactly what I do not need. A lot of feelings and emotions surface once again. I am trying to keep them under control because I do not want to tuck my feelings away again. During this time, Mickey is making his move on Nadera, and he is successful. While waiting at the car, I look back to see her kissing my cousin. My heart sinks as Brick's advice quickly surfaces: Don't trust these women! They can be more scandalous and treacherous than a man!

After witnessing this, I understand what Brick was trying to explain.

I am very quiet when we pull away from Nadera's house. I keep thinking this girl has been lying to me. Nadera told me over and over she loves me. I cannot help but think if she loved me, why treat me in this manner. My cousin is talking about something, but I am not listening. As I focus in on what he is saying, the kiss does not mean anything to him because he is talking about Leslie's friend. It then dawns on me this predicament is my fault. I should have swallowed my pride and told my cousin the truth about my feelings for Nadera. The sin known as pride is a part of the love game. You learn to win by losing and this is a big loss to me. I will charge this loss to the game of love.

"Do you want to know why I tried to kiss Nadera? I needed to show you that you need to focus your attention elsewhere. Homer, you have a beautiful girl waiting to see you." Mickey states as he reminds me about Leslie.

"Yeah, you are right, Mickey. I need to focus my attention elsewhere. I am glad the truth surfaced. I am still hurt, but I see now I must move beyond this fantasy in my head." I state somberly.

My sorrows are quickly tucked away once Mickey peps me up about seeing Leslie. I have Mickey swing by my house so I can get some condoms just in case. He wants to take a quick shower because we have been running around the city all day.

"Are you going back out tonight, Homer?" my mother asks while I am in the shower.

"We were headed back to dad's house. I will probably stay with him tonight." I yell back through the bathroom door.

Mickey phones his father at my dad's house to tell them he will stay at my house. We are covered to have all night to do what we please.

We arrive at Leslie's friend's house. We are surprised to find the girls are home alone. I want to make sure it is okay to come in because I do not want any surprises. She informs us her parents are out of town. Mickey immediately gives me a firm pat on my shoulder as a thank you because this is what he wanted this weekend. Leslie and I go to a different part of the house so we can talk. She leads me to the screened-in back patio area. The girl's house is nice. I can tell her folks are making a good living.

"I need to tell you something about the day I met your ex-boyfriend." I state to Leslie.

"I already know about what happened at the party with Nadera. Therefore, we broke up. He did not know my cousin witnessed the entire event." Leslie interrupts.

"Damn, what a small world."

"I admit I have been intrigued by you when I saw you at a football game early in the school year. I do not think it is coincidence we met a few days after the party."

"That's all I needed to hear, Leslie. How can we make this relationship work over the summer being at two different schools and living in different areas of town?"

"It probably will not work. We can be special friends. It will be easier for the both of us to date each other and see other people."

"I think I can work with this agreement." I respond with a smile.

Leslie wants to lay down due to being up all day. I need to lie down because Mickey and I have also been up all day attending my great uncle's funeral. We go to ask her friend where we can rest because he is in her room with Mickey. Before we knock on the door, we hear moaning and groaning coming from the room. Based on these noises, I take it Mickey's wish is being fulfilled. Leslie and I decide to lie on the couch in the den area. We watch TV for a moment and kiss for a while. Leslie is willing to let me explore her as far as I like. Things almost go in my favor, but we both fall asleep from being so tired. I wake up thinking we need to leave. In a sleepy voice, Leslie informs me we are good, so I lay back down.

Leslie and I have this type of relationship throughout high school. There are numerous nights we sleep in the same bed as special friends either at my house or hers.

Hole 14 – Breeze of Life

Even though school is out for the summer, it does not seem like a vacation. I start by playing in a golf tournament my high school coach registered us to play in Dallas. Since I am fifteen, my coach signs me up to play in the thirteen to fifteen-year-old age group in hopes of me placing high playing against a younger field. I am furious because I know I can play with the sixteen to eighteen-year-olds.

The tournament is held over four days. The first two days are the team events. The last two days are match play individual format. We play thirty-six holes each day for the first two days. It will be tough because it is unseasonably hotter than normal in Texas during the summer. We knew it would be hot, but the heat indexes for the first two days are over to the hundred-and-ten-degree range for the early part of June. We drink water every chance we get, but it still does not help. We have guys vomiting on the course from the heat due to trying to rush down fluids after a match to make sure they are hydrated for the next round.

During our afternoon round on the first day, we are lucky enough to get a scattered thunderstorm. I am in the last group with my playing partner with five holes remaining to close out the day. As the storm starts to form, the shade from the clouds feels like an arctic breeze. We play the last holes with decent scores to place in the championship round.

I am on the seventeenth green when the skies open and rain starts to pour on the course. Most of the players are either running in the rain or lying on the grass as it rains. A few of the snobbish players try to hide under the trees with their umbrellas like the water will make them melt. There are some steps leading to the eighteenth tee box I sit on to take in the moment. As I look around, it dawns on me I am the only minority I see on the playing field. Of course, no one knows the difference because of my outer appearance. As I survey the field again, I do not like the feeling of being the only one. I begin to feel out of place and lonely. The rain only lasts for about ten minutes. The storm does not produce enough water to stop play.

As I tee off on hole number eighteen, I feel a cool breeze rushing through my body instead of against it. The last time I felt like this was right after my fight with Slick. I remember staring at myself as I walk to my ball. I finally understand I am halting my personal growth. I need to change my mindset from 'trying to be something' to the attitude of 'I am something.' I realize even if I fail, I succeeded because I tried. Most of the guys where I come from are always striving to be something they are not because of pressure from peers. They are afraid to try because of fear of failure. I need to disregard trying to fit in and resist fighting my feelings. I feel like a dirty diamond being pulled from the mine. I need to have the carbon, dirt, and the other minerals removed. I need shaping, cutting, and polishing to become a beautiful jewel. After everything I have experienced up to this point in my life, I feel like I am fresh from the mine heading for cleaning. I know I am a work in progress. I recognize I need to put in some more work to evolve further. I feel so enlightened, I do not care that I end up making a bogey on the last hole. Because of the play of the other members on my team, we cannot finish any higher than fourth, even if I made an eagle on the hole.

While sitting in the clubhouse waiting on the next day's schedule, I am told I have a high seeding in the match play rounds. My coach sends me over to registration table to get all my paperwork submitted before we leave for the hotel. One of tournament officials informs me my age is not on her sheet. I notice some of the competition in the my field. I feel I will not gain anything by playing against these guys. I lie by stating I am sixteen. I really want to see where my game stands against the big boys. I see my coach coming to the table; so, I quickly sign my paperwork before he realizes what I have done. I know he will force me to play in my age group.

When my coach finds out I am playing up in age, he is furious. Fortunately for me, it is too late to make changes. While my coach is fussing at me all the way to the bus, I am reading the rules of the tournament. I find a rule which clearly states a player can play up in age but cannot go down in an age group.

"What were you thinking, Homer? You could have easily made it to the championship round in this field." Coach states after I show him the rule in writing.

"I like a challenge and winning is not important to me. I want to prove to myself I can compete on a high level. It is about personal growth more so than getting a trophy. I would rather gain my competitor's respect than look at a trophy collecting dust on a shelf."

He respects my view but punishes me by making me clean all the players' clubs before the next day's round. I do not mind the punishment because I am motivated by the challenge I will face tomorrow. Once I am finished, I call my grandfather to tell him about the tournament, including what I discovered about myself walking to my ball on the eighteenth green. My grandfather lets me know he is proud of me and to make sure I have the same conversation with my mother. I call my mother to tell her everything. She gives me the same lecture as my coach, except it is for being stubborn.

"Nadera left a message on the answering machine." My mother adds. "Is it for you or me?"

My mother really likes Nadera, but I don't think she knows what transpired between us.

"I called her already. She left the message for you. You need to call her when you get off the phone with me. Use the calling card I gave you. Just don't talk too long."

"I don't think I can because I am flying high on adrenaline. I don't want anything to distract me from my main objective. I do not have time for a rollercoaster ride right now."

"I said, call her, boy!" my mother states aggressively.

After I hang up with my mother, I start to think about Nadera. I want to call her and spill everything I am feeling. However, I am afraid because I just can't handle any form of rejection at this time. I talk to Leslie, but it is a quick conversation. Leslie knows how bad I want to prove myself at this tournament. She wants to lend me her ear but is too busy to talk.

I go ahead and call Nadera because I am tired of holding in my feelings. Her sister is on the phone and will not relinquish her call even after I state I am calling long distance. I give her the number to my room just in case she wants to call me back.

My roommate for the week is on his way down to the lobby to eat dinner. I will join them once I take a shower. After two rounds in the heat carrying my golf bag, I am tired, and my muscles are starting to cramp. I relieve myself in the restroom before getting in the shower. Before I flush the toilet, I always look at my urine to see if it is the right color after being in the heat. I notice something is wrong when my urine looks dark orange. My body is dehydrated. I drink a glass of water from the bathroom sink and it is terrible. However, I need to get some fluids in my system before my muscles shut down. This is the last thing I need because I do not want to stay up half the night getting myself hydrated. I need the sleep. I stay in the shower for about thirty minutes.

Once I clean up, I make my way to the lobby where everyone is eating dinner. I tell my coach I think I am dehydrated. We quickly jump in the van and head to a convenience store to buy some Gatorade. Coach purchases a case of water for everyone to share. Once we get back to the hotel, he gives the whole team two bottles and asks the manager if any fruit is available. He wants to see the bottles empty before he calls lights out for the evening. I don't eat anything for dinner because I am worried about staying hydrated. It is still early as the team gathers in Coach's room to play around and go over the day's events. I ask to be excused because I want to lie down. The guys on my team are cool, but they are all Caucasian boys. I do not feel comfortable being around them in this type of setting.

Once I make it to my room, I see the light blinking, indicating we have messages. The front desk informs me my roommate's mother and Nadera called. I down a bottle of Gatorade and another water before calling. Nadera answers and we exchange greetings.

"I was thinking about you, Homer. How are things going?"

I pass her concern off as bullshit.

"I need to get some things off my chest before we go on." I state before going into my dialogue about what happened to me on the golf course today.

"The breeze is God's way of talking to you and sending down a blessing."

"I did not think of it this way. The last time this happened, I met you a few days later."

"What else is on your mind, Homer?"

"You really hurt me the night we broke up. I was not upset about you kissing some other guy. I felt you could have been honest about it when we talked earlier in the day."

"Homer, the whole thing was blown out of context. He kissed me. What you did not see was me pushing him off me."

"Yeah right, it took a few moments to resist him in front of everyone," I state sarcastically sue to feeling this is another bullshit answer.

"I do not want us to fight right now."

"Why did you kiss my cousin? This is something I do not understand."

"You treated me like I was nothing to you. It was a farce to show you I also have moved on. I wanted to teach you a lesson to not be so stubborn about your feelings. I know how you feel about me. I can see it in your eyes. I feel the same way about you. It is time to lay everything out on the table." Nadera expresses sincerely.

"It would have been easier to tell me than play me against my cousin. If feelings are what you want, then here is how I feel. I unconditionally love you. Our breakup affected me to the point where I probably will never expose myself to anyone like this again. Knowing you do not feel the same about me based on some of your actions is what hurts the most." I state passionately.

Nadera is quiet during my explanation. I take the silence as my point was not getting across. Since she is not responding, I am about to end the conversation to focus on making sure I am hydrated and mentally prepare myself for tomorrow.

"I love you, Homer." Nadera expresses catching me off guard.

"If those are not just words, then I love you too, Nadera."

This is the extent of the conversation. I do not talk to Nadera any more during the summer. I feel relieved my feelings are out there and not repressed in my heart. I want to follow up with Nadera after this conversation to see where it may lead, but I am not going to set myself up to be hurt by her again. Getting over her is too painful.

The next day is quite eventful on the golf course. Since the field consists of about seventy players, we do a shotgun start to ensure all the matches are played. I start on the sixteenth hole. Since it is a long walk, I put my clubs on my back and start my journey. I find it unusual that some kids get rides, and some don't.

I finally find another minority in the crowd. He is a young kid about thirteen years of age. He is tall for his age with the most intriguing disposition. We are heading in the same direction, so I strike up a conversation with him. He is going to the fourteenth hole. He introduces himself as Eric. I can tell this kid is not the typical thirteen-year-old golfer. This kid is analyzing the course as we are walking and talking. He is looking at the type of sand in the bunkers, the height of the first cut of rough, and the slopes of the fairways. I am glad this kid is in the thirteen- to fifteen-year-old group. I figure the only way he will lose is if he beats himself. We exchange 'good lucks' and I thank him for the pointers during our walk.

I introduce myself and shake hands with the other players upon arriving to the tee box where I will start my day.

"Were you giving that kid a hard time?" My opponent asks after we shake hands.

"No. We were conversing about the course."

"You should have because niggers do not belong here."

"Forgive me, but I am not following what you are saying."

"This is a white man's game. A nigger does not need to be on the course unless he is carrying a bag or tending to the grounds." My opponent states without tact.

I immediately want to take one of my woods to this kid's brain, but you can't do that in golf since it is a gentlemen's game. I look over at the official because I know he hears this guy's comments. The official just ignores it and goes about telling us the rules. I am seeing red because I want to crush this kid. I hear a soft voice tell me to use my head. When I shake my opponent's hand, I give him a grin and advise him this match will not last long.

I win the coin toss and allow my opponent to tee off first. My opponent is trying to show off his distance from the tee by attempting to crush a ball down the fairway with his brand-new shiny driver. He overcompensates on his swing, hitting his ball into the rough. My uncle taught me early that this game is played from the green back to the tee box instead of the tee box to the green.

"A good short game will benefit you better than trying to see how far you can hit the ball." I can hear my uncle telling me from Memphis.

While teeing my ball up, the breeze I felt on the eighteenth green yesterday suddenly emerges. I hit my worn down three wood down the center of the fairway about fifty yards shorter than my opponent. I can hear him snickering under his breath. While planning my second shot before I reach my ball, I realize I am a full six iron distance away from the green. When I hit my shot, I know it is a good one. I hit it a little firm because there is still some moisture on the ground, preventing the ball from rolling on the green if I hit it short. As it lands on the green, it stops immediately, leaving me with an eighteen-foot putt for birdie. My opponent is in much worse shape. His ball is buried and on a slope. At this age, I know he does not have the skillset to make it to the green with a shot in this type of scenario. I can tell by my opponent's demeanor he is going to go for the green. I have seen this numerous times. A player believes he has the skillset to make a difficult shot and falls short. As predicted, his ball sprays across the fairway into the rough about forty yards short of the green. I can tell by his body language he is flustered. He hits his next shot over the green. All I need to do is make par to win the hole. I do better than par by making a birdie to go one up. Fortunately for me, my opponent never gets on track. I end up winning the match after I am up four holes after the fifteenth hole.

"Not bad for a nigger who doesn't belong here." I state as we shake hands.

The look on his face is priceless because he is fooled by the camouflage of my skin. I bump into Eric as he is coming in the locker room between matches. He lets me know he won his match by seven holes. Even though this is impressive, I am not surprised because I know this kid is good.

My next opponent is a little tougher. The match comes down to a decisive par putt on the eighteenth hole to determine a winner. The only difference in the match is a missed birdie opportunity on the thirteenth hole by my opponent. Because of the error, I tie the match on the fifteenth hole. Instead of my opponent being up by one hole playing the eighteenth, we are tied. He misses his par putt on eighteen. I know if the match is extended, I will probably lose because I am running low on energy. I am also mentally exhausted. My putt is only about four feet, but it is a tricky one. It reminds me of the ninth hole at Pine Hill I play regularly at home with my uncle and Brick. I use my knowledge of this green to line up the putt. If I do not hit it perfect, it will go past the hole down a slope about ten feet to the right. I play it a few degrees to the left and just make it in on the right side of the cup. This is a relief. I do not think people know about the mental side of golf. It wears you down worse than the physical aspect of the game. After shaking my opponent's hand, I feel the mild summer breeze across my body. With this victory, I am in the quarter final round.

I make it past my quarter final opponent with ease. The downside to the victory is my pitching wedge being bent from a shot out of the woods. Due to my next opponent destroying his foe, I do not have time to attempt to get it fixed or have it replaced with a teammate's club. My roommate also wins his match. While preparing for my semifinal round, I find out my next opponent is Eric. Eric uses the same clause in the rules I did to move up a level. We talk a bit while we wait on the first hole.

"Are you having problems with the players on the field?" I ask.

"They talk a little trash. I try to embarrass the ones who talk the most junk. I heard about your first opponent yesterday. I appreciate what you did. I am immune to the ignorance being the outcast on the course." Eric replies.

"I feel your pain. I am usually the only outcast on the course. Your appearance stands out more than mine."

"I can tell by our conversation yesterday we fit the same mold." Eric replies as we both laugh.

Eric is also of mixed heritage. Fortunately for him, he looks like he is African American.

"I bent my pitching wedge coming out of the woods. I need to figure out how to hit it with the shaft bent." I share with Eric.

"The way it is bent will cause a natural draw. Try to aim it more right of the target." Eric advises as his dad arrives.

We talk a bit while we are waiting for the match in front of us to clear the green. We explain to his father the context of our conversation. Eric's father reminds me of my uncle. He provides some deep insight about what we can expect from some of the players on the course.

"This is still a white man's game. Believe me when I tell you they are not willing to give it up to minorities. I am not just talking black and white. I am referencing any nationality who does not look Caucasian. They will try to get into your mind by calling you out of your name. They will search for any advantage to throw you off mentally. Minorities have tried for decades to do what you are doing now. Both of you have a chance to do something special." Eric's father express harshly and bluntly.

"Sir, how do we overcome this behavior while not wanting to retaliate? I mean, we are far away from the sixties of racial injustice. I feel as though I am equal to these guys, and I should be judged by my play more so than my ethnic makeup."

"Oh, young man you have a lot to learn! We are not as far away from the sixties and racial injustice as you think. We are still in a dark time. However, you answered your own question about how to retaliate. Use this ball, these clubs, and your mind to defeat these guys or any injustices you encounter while playing. If you make them respect your skills, then you have won the battle. If you learn to ignore the ignorance and disrespect them by dominating them while playing their game, then you will win the war." Eric's father replies.

The conversation with Eric's father blows me away. I never thought about approaching golf or life in this manner.

When Eric tees off, I know I am in trouble. This kid has the perfect golf swing. The game seems like it comes natural to him. We stay tied for about seven holes until he begins to break away on number eight. I know I will struggle on the next few holes because they are short ones. I will need my pitching wedge on some approach shots. I try to justify not using my wedge by hitting irons off the tee to setup possibly using my eight or nine iron so I can take a full swing on my approach shots. This strategy does not work because Eric's game is at a pinnacle. When I make a birdie, Eric makes one causing us to halve the hole, rebuffing my attempts to gain ground. By the time we make it to number fourteen, I am five holes down. I need to win all five holes in order to extend the match. This feat is impossible. I can tell Eric wants to end the match, but I thwart his plan by making a few birdies.

The fourteenth hole is a par three. Eric's tee shot almost goes in but lips out the cup leaving him with about four feet for a definite birdie. The only way to extend the match to the next hole is to make a hole in one. Uh-oh, talk about pressure. To make matters worse, the green is about one hundred and ten yards. However, the distance to the cup is only about ninety-eight yards. The only shot I know how to play from this distance is my pitching wedge. I cannot aim it left because of a green side bunker and water is to the right. I have to hit my pitching wedge because I am not good enough to control the distance on my nine iron at seventy-five percent.

I hit my pitching wedge aiming about fifteen degrees towards the water. The ball draws like Eric and I discussed earlier. However, the ball hits the right side of the green too hot and rolls to the left side leaving me about a thirty-foot putt for birdie. I still have a shot if Eric misses his putt. A four-foot putt the way he is playing is a given. I give my putt a good, firm stroke, but it I push it past the cup by three feet. I concede the hole after I miss the putt. Eric shakes my hand and puts his arm around my shoulder as we walk to our bags. I start to tear up a bit because I am disappointed in my play. I feel like I didn't prove anything by losing in the semifinal round. I wipe my tears away on my golf towel.

"Homer, you are a first-class opponent. Your birdies frustrated me because you would not let me finish the match earlier. I like the way you adapted to your club being bent. You did not allow it to hinder your play. I know we will meet again in the future." Eric states as my coach makes his way up to us.

"You proved more to yourself by moving up a level and making it to the semifinal round. You beat some real quality opponents Homer!" Coach expresses.

"How old are you, Homer?" Eric's dad asks.

"Fifteen, sir, but I will turn sixteen at the end of the summer." I reply.

Eric is shocked I am only fifteen because I look older than my age.

"If you keep playing like you just played, I guarantee you will be playing on the next level with ease. What is your full name so I can keep tabs on you?" Eric's father states to me.

I talk to Eric and his dad all the way back to the clubhouse. By the time we make it back, I am over the loss.

My roommate also lost. He receives the third-place medal because he only loses by two holes. I get the fourth-place medal. We also get our team medals for coming in fourth overall.

"Homer, I just found out Eric is the top junior golfer in his age group." Coach informs me before we leave the course.

"In my opinion, he is the top junior golfer under the age of seventeen in the country." I add.

"Hey guys, listen up. Overall, this was a positive trip. We played well against some good competition. Some college recruiters inquired about some of you. I gave them your information so they can keep track of your development." Coach informs the group.

As we pack the van for the long ride home, I feel like I turn a corner in my life during this trip. While placing my clubs and luggage in the van, I feel the breeze again as I board. The breeze is the validation stamp to close out the trip.

Hole 15 – Some Degree of Freedom

Once I return home, I finish my baseball season before going to see my grandparents. Our summer trips are shorter due to me and my sister getting older. My sister is heading into her senior year of high school and struggling to make her college decision. Over the summer she is trying to get everything together to begin her senior year while working and maintaining a social life. Whatever time I can get with my grandparents is good enough for me because I cherish their company.

Due to coming off a good summer of golf, I make sure I take my clubs with me to Petersburg so I can practice. I want to train a lot and I am fortunate my grandfather enjoys walking the course with me in the afternoons. He takes this time to get some exercise. I am benefiting due to the good course work to increase my golf IQ. We have some good conversations about life. I confess to him the relationships I am having with girls and how my heart belongs to Nadera. We talk about sexual intercourse. I come clean about the girls with whom I've had a sexual relationship.

"I think I did it more so out of curiosity than caring about these girls. I am nowhere near being active with the person I want. Nadera is also a good friend. We can talk about anything, we cry together, and pray sometimes." I explain to my grandfather, omitting the downside of our relationship.

"Right now, you guys are looking to see where you fit regarding what you like. You now have received the blueprint of how you want to be loved. You want every new person you meet to make you feel like she makes you feel. Right now, this is all a game. Both of you are curious. This curiosity is making you look at different women. You try to like them because you want to know whether you are compatible to this type of person. It is not a bad thing because it is better to shop around before you make a final purchase. Nadera is doing the same thing, she loves you, but she is curious. One day, your heart will set her free. If it is truly meant to be, then you and Nadera will meet back up again. Until then, keep piecing the woman of your dreams together." my grandfather states with sincerity.

"How did you know that is what I am doing?"

"I did the same thing before I met your grandmother!" he states with a grin.

My grandfather takes note of my game on the golf course. He is impressed with the progression of my skill set. I overhear him telling my mother I have a gift. I think my baseball game is better, but he points out my golf game is special. He has my uncle start talking to me about college recruiting to understand the ins and outs of the process.

"Homer, would you consider coming to college in Virginia if you have the opportunity?"

"I wouldn't mind, Grandpa, because I will be closer to you. I have my coach's information at the house if they want my stats or whatever is needed." I reply enthusiastically.

My grandfather finalizes my driver training during the summer by letting me drive him wherever we are going. I figure if I can get his seal of approval, it will be easier for my mother to let me get my license and drive. Because of my schedule back home, I miss the free driver's education classes offered during the summer. I am fortunate enough to get into a class at the local high school where my uncle is the head football coach. My grandmother pays the fees. By the time we leave to return home, I have my certification. There is a drawback. Since I completed the class in Virginia, the insurance company will not allow the premium discount since I live in Tennessee. It is not a big issue because I am already signed up to take driver's ED at school during the fall. Until I complete the class, I must pay a good chunk of my car insurance.

School starts a few weeks before my sixteenth birthday. I am riding with my sister in the mornings. I have to wait on my mother to pick me up after school because of golf practice. I am riding to the driving range and the course we practice on with my coach. During the evenings and weekends, I am riding out with Gold or Bronze because they already have their licenses and cars.

Mine and Silver's birthdays are four days apart. We are both anxiously waiting for our day to come. On the morning of my birthday, I miss the first half of school to go to the DMV to take my driver's test. I pressure my mom to get me on her insurance immediately as my birthday gift because I am ready to drive. I already have a part-time job lined up who are willing to work around my golf schedule.

Later in the afternoon, my dad surprises me with letting me drive one of his cars during the week. The downside is I must give it back to him for the weekends. My mom buys a new two seat car she ends up driving every day. My sister and I fight for the second car on the weekends.

Now that I am driving, I am feeling a sense of freedom. Coach is a little flexible by allowing us about an hour and a half to get to practices. School is letting out at two fifteen and practice does not start until three thirty. Coach tries to sell this time to use in study hall to do our homework, but I think he knows he is dealing with some hormonal teenagers. I use this time to hang out after school to relax my mind a bit from being in class for the last seven hours. Since I am in my junior year, the classes are getting tougher. I have Honors Biology, Honors Calculus, Honors English, Honors World History, Psychology, Drivers ED and Music. My English teacher makes it clear our entire first semester is devoted to a term paper on our topic of choice. Biology is like learning to do surgery daily. Psychology is cool because my golf coach is the teacher. My teacher for calculus is the hardest teacher ever, including the professors I have in college. This dude takes your mind through a rollercoaster ride every day for fifty-five minutes. I struggle in his class because it is right before lunch. I need to take a class like this during first period or after lunch because it is too brutal. I am not struggling with the material. I am struggling with mental focus.

Due to state athletic guidelines, golf starts earlier in the school year so the regular season is completed by the end of September. This year, our season is extended because we win our district, compete in the city tournament, and qualify for the state championship. I am playing great golf as an individual player. We mostly came in first or second as a team. My overall individual score always put me in first place. Because of the summer tournament, I am already in the recruiting database. I start getting mail from schools interested in me attending their institutions. Due to my play before the city tournament, I am getting phone calls at the house from colleges. By the end of the district tournament, I have visits from coaches and scholarship offers on the table.

Due to my workload at school, golf, and trying to keep a part-time job, I am spreading myself very thin. I am not sleeping much due to talking to recruiters and trying to get my schoolwork done afterwards. I am getting into bed at about one or two in the morning during the week. I am taking over-the-counter pills to keep myself up and running while also abusing alcohol and weed to relax a bit. My grades are suffering more so from lack of rest rather than not knowing the material. Recruiters often visiting during my lunch hour during school. Even though they are interrupting my only social time, they bring some good food. Some schools are attempting underhanded tactics to get me to sign. My uncle made me aware of this and advised me over the summer to not sign or make a commitment until I visit the school.

I do talk to Aimee and Leslie on occasions. I am fortunate Aimee is in all my Honors classes. I can reach out to her when I am struggling. Aimee has her own phone line, making her able to help me out very late. I often go to Aimee's house very late to copy the notes. Aimee's room is located on the front side of her house, far away from her mother's room. I get caught in Aimee's room one night by her mother. She does not freak out or anything because we are studying. Her mother does not mind me coming over late. She just tells me to come through the front door instead of the window. All I need are the class notes to catch up. Since golf lasts right until the first report card period, I do not have to worry about my grades. I mean, I want to keep them high enough where I do not have to dig myself out of a hole during the remaining of the school year.

Nadera and I are still friends. We talk at school when we see each other. She can tell when I am having a hard time trying to balance everything. She is the only one I will get off the phone for even if I am talking to recruiters from a college. I am not dating anyone seriously because I do not have time to court or take them out. Even if I can tell a girl is interested in me, I will not request the girl's number or give out my phone number because I do not have time to call them.

When I am at home on the weekends, I often ask Nadera to grab a bite to eat or catch a movie. I know Nadera is dating other guys, but she never declines any of my invitations. During this time, I become fond of going to the movies because it is a dark place where no one can bother you for a few hours. I eventually start going by myself just to get away for a moment. If Nadera asks me to do anything, I alter my plans to accommodate her requests. This is the only time I can be alone with someone and tell the truth about how I am feeling. It is like we are still in a relationship because we hold hands and kiss each other. Overall, we are real good friends. No matter the circumstance, we can always count on each other. Nadera is battling her own personal issues as well. I think we both use each other to escape our realities, even if it is only for a few hours. I tell her everything about recruiting and the school pressure I am feeling. I tell her about the pills, alcohol, and weed keeping me going. She slaps the hell out of me when I tell her. I believe her and her mother think I am telling Nadera this to gain sympathy, but it is guilt driving my confession.

"I can't see you like this, Homer. Are you high now? Are you under the influence of something while driving?" Nadera yells.

"Right now, at this moment, no, I am not high. The pills are to wake me up. The alcohol is at night to relax me. The weed is sporadic. I never do anything when I know. Never mind Nadera, I should have kept my mouth closed. I was just laying down my burdens. That's fine if this is how you want things to be between us. Something told me you would not understand."

"You never do anything when you know what, Homer?'

"I never do anything when I know I am going to see you. Right now, I look forward to seeing you more than ever. I never want you to see me under the influence of anything because I never want you to have a negative impression of me. I know you are dating other guys, but I need you more than ever right now. Everything is so complex. I need to hear you tell me I love you. Those words and your presence make this frustrating time a hell of a lot easier." I yell as the tone of the conversation quickly goes from yelling to calm.

"What if I tell your mother?"

"Go ahead, she will not understand either." I reply before pulling out of Nadera's driveway.

Leslie is still in the picture. She is just as busy as I am, but we always link up when we have the chance. Her mom goes out of town quite often, leaving her to watch her little brother. This isn't considered child endangerment because Leslie is sixteen. By law, she is old enough to be responsible for his wellbeing. On some weekends, I go over her house just to hang out. It is relaxing sitting with her brother, playing video games. Leslie is very intelligent. She is already getting college credits for the classes she takes as a junior in high school. I am taking advantage of her knowledge to keep my grades up in my classes. Leslie lets me do something at her house I badly need. Leslie lets me sleep.

Even though I do not have a curfew, I make sure I come home at a decent time. When I work on the weekends, I tell my mom I am working until midnight at the grocery store. Since I am under eighteen, I cannot work past nine o'clock. When I leave work, I go to Leslie's house, since she is close by. Even though we come close to having sex on some nights, we never commit to the act. I use Silver's house as a cover up. I tell my mother we are going to a party after I get off work and will stay at his house overnight. Part of this is true. I shower, change clothes, and pick Silver up from his house. I drop him off after our outing and then head across town to Leslie's house for the night. I am a good kid who has gained my mother's trust. She knows I am not an angel. However, I will not do anything to land myself in any trouble.

We also hang out at Gold's house. His house is in a rough area of town, but he has a loving home. Gold's mom always has something pleasant to say. She talks to us like we are her own children. Gold's grandmother is the highlight of our visits. She is funny with the advice she gives us about girls. Even though her approach is awkward, her advice is on point. We often sit on his front porch to chill out for a moment before we hit the streets.

Silver does not live too far from Gold. Silver's grandfather is like Gold's grandmother. He talks to us— mostly making fun of how we look. I think he gets a thrill out of it especially when it comes to Bronze. Silver's grandfather was a pretty good golfer in his day. I enjoy sitting with him talking about the game. When a golf tournament is on TV, he often quizzes me about what to do in the situation the golfer we are watching is facing. He also knows I am dating Silver's cousin, Nadera, which is his niece. He jokingly gives me a hard time about how Nadera is wasting her time with me.

Gold, Silver, and I are sharing a similar upbringing by being in households without fathers present. Bronze's predicament is the definition of an American family. He lives with his mother and father in a community like mine. We all start to bond when at the young age of twelve. The bond is continuing to grow as we become young men trying to figure out what direction to follow.

By statistics standards, we fall into three categories because of the zip codes where we live. One of the main classifiers is due to being raised by single black mothers. We are slated to fall into three categories, which consists of going to jail, becoming homosexuals, or dead by the time we are twenty-five. From a societal standard, we are more likely to end up in the penal system.

182

Due to God's grace, we all have interventions, which assist our transition to hardworking honest men. Gold has a teacher who makes sure he is enrolled in the gifted program during junior high, which leads him to our college preparatory high school. Silver has his grandfather and uncle to guide him down the same path. I have my grandfather, uncles, cousins, Dre', and Brick to make sure I stay on a straight and narrow path. We also have wonderful mothers who are doing the best they can regarding raising boys. I know it is a difficult task for mine. They deserve a lot of praise. I hope one day these types of success stories are added to the statistics.

Finally, golf season is over, allowing me to slow down a bit. We lose in the first round of the state as a team, but I qualify for the individual tournament in the spring. I get back on track with my grades and my social life is getting a lot better. I lose my job at the grocery store due to recruiting visits. After visiting numerous schools, I narrow my choices down to about five universities. My mother is skeptical about a few of my choices because she wants to make sure I get my education. She emphasizes her reasons for not attending the local university in town. She wants my sister and me to experience life away from home.

The schools on my list are exceptional universities. All except one has a nationally ranked golf program. All the schools except for one have their own golf courses, which rivals any course I have played during my brief golf experiences. The one school with the exception on my list is an up-and-coming program some analysts consider a long shot for me to sign because of my skill set and notoriety. However, the coach is a good guy. He impresses my mother and me during his visit to the house. His goal is to build a powerhouse program from the bottom. I will be the school's biggest recruit who will get the program rolling in the right direction. The only thing holding me up from signing at one of these schools is my ACT and SAT scores.

The top school on my list requires a twenty-four on the ACT to get accepted. The coach advises me he can work around this if I score between an eighteen and twenty-three. This is my mother's least favorite choice because she considers the school too big and too far away from home. After talking with my guidance counselor, she suggests I join some organizations who do community service work to make my entrance resume more impressive. She gives me a list and I am immediately drawn to an organization backed by a National Greek Organization where Dre' is a member. I immediately approach him about joining and a letter of recommendation. A few weeks' later, after the interviews and information sessions, I am a member of the organization. This is like being in a college Greek fraternity. We elect officers, attend meetings, and community service projects are mandatory.

They teach us how to work and play hard. Our biggest fundraisers are the parties we coordinate. We have members from schools from around the city. We must choose venues that can accommodate over a thousand people. Each venue is filled to capacity. If you are late, you probably end up paying triple the entry price. We attract so many girls some guys do not have a problem paying the inflated entry fee. Of course, with having members of different schools in one location, a fight always pops off either inside the party or in the parking lot. The college guys make sure we do not get involved with any of the violence. They make us stay inside until the police clear the area.

I get into a few arguments due to some girl's boyfriend getting jealous. They figure they can take me down easily because of my skin tone. Since the girls are approaching me, my suggestion to the guys is to take their frustrations out with the girls.

184

I develop a reputation as a playboy because I am dating girls from all the different schools. All I am doing is talking to them. I spend most of my time during parties dancing with Aimee, Lisa, and a few other girls who are just my friends. Because these girls are drop dead gorgeous, the playboy rumors take off. I am the furthest thing from a playboy. I don't think people know how much time I spend alone with the demons I am battling. I hate being alone because this is when I am tempted by the demons of gluttony, lust, anger, and pride. I can fight off these demons while I am focusing on athletics, school, Nadera, hanging with Gold, Silver, Bronze and deciding on college choices. However, when there is quiet time in my bedroom, I am tempted by the demons with all the sins haunting me.

Hole 16 – Controlling my Sins

The night before I take my ACT, some of my sister's friends are hanging out at the house. A few guys bring some drinks, so I participate with them to ease the pressure of taking the test in the morning.

Some of us smoke for a bit in the backyard. I go to bed about ten thirty because I must be at the testing location at eight thirty. I have to leave about seven because I promise Gold I will pick him up at seven thirty. When I get to my room, my sister's friend, Crystal, is lying in my bed under the covers talking to her boyfriend. Crystal and I are in the same class, but she hangs out with the older crowd. Even though we know each other from school, we never really communicate or hang out. I am high as hell, but I do not have her leave. Crystal stays in the bed, continuing her conversation under the covers while I fall asleep over the covers. Once again, my ego wants to tell you we have blazing sex, but we sleep like cousins in the same bed.

I wake up about two in the morning and notice the house is clear except for another one of Elise's friends having sex with some guy in her bed. She is loud and yelling like she has found the Holy Ghost at church. Before I get downstairs to get something to drink, I hear a cry of "Why did you hit me?" coming from the den. Some drunken guy slaps my sister because she will not have sex with him. I immediately go after

186

this guy. After a few slams against the wall, I notice he is too drunk to fight back. His friend rushes downstairs because of the commotion. This guy is an officer in the organization I belong.

"Homer, let him go! Right now!" his friend orders like I am supposed to do as he says.

"Man, fuck you! He slapped my sister. What would you do if he hit your sister? If he can't defend himself then I will give you what he deserves." I reply.

"Homer, please let him go." My sister, Elise, yells.

She knows how I am when I get angry. The guy backs down. I politely tell both to get the hell out of our house. I am nice enough to help this drunken bastard to the car. I drag him up the stairs, intentionally hitting his head on every step.

By the time his friend gets dressed, he has a few knots on his head and a swollen jaw. I can tell he is upset but he knows I am not going to back down from him if he wants to defend his friend's honor. I politely push the drunk through the front door, causing him to fall off the front porch.

"Homer, you are wrong for what you are doing." My sister's friend expresses.

"Shut up! This is personal. He crossed the line when he slapped Elise. Don't stand out here acting as though you care so much about this guy. You are upset because I interrupted your so-called intimacy session with a guy who really doesn't give a shit about you at all. You are a stupid, sex graved, imbecile. You are welcome to leave with them. See if he cares enough for you to give you a ride home." I yell to my sister's friend from the front porch.

We wake up a few neighbors because we are yelling loud.

"Don't worry, Homer. We will get you back for this. We owe you one." The officer in my organization threatens as he drives off.

The next morning, I am off to take my ACT test. Gold and I arrive about twenty minutes early. I should be hungover from the night before, but my adrenaline flowing from what happened a few hours earlier is offsetting my high. In my opinion, the test is hard. I feel it has nothing to do with the knowledge I have acquired during my twelve years in school.

"Just relax, Homer. You are too worried about getting the score you need to get in your top university choice." Gold states during a break as Nadera walks up.

"Don't worry, Homer. Calm down and you will do just fine." Nadera states as she gently touches me on my back.

"This is what I have been telling this idiot all morning." Gold adds.

"Dang, Gold, seeing her, touching me on my back, and those few words make all the difference. We are going to have to talk seriously after the test. I want us to rekindle our relationship. I am playing games with all the other girls."

"Homer, it is about time you got some freaking sense and go after what you really want." Gold states clearly to me.

I struggle to get through the test, but I am more relaxed. I am ecstatic to turn in my answer sheet when the test is over. I know I will end up taking the test again, but this is the farthest thing from my mind. I see Nadera and Gold talking, but I am delayed getting to them because I bump into a kid I play against on our rival high school golf team. We discuss the test for a moment until he asks me if I have made my decision on what school I am attending. He is a senior who has signed to play with one of the schools on my list. He is trying to acquire some brownie points with his coach by informing him of my intentions. I let him know I have narrowed it down to five schools, but I do not tell him which ones.

I finally make my way up to Gold, but Nadera is gone.

"Homer, you need to ask Nadera if she needs a ride home." Gold whispers to me.

"How will you get home?" I ask.

"I can get to the house. Just ask her. This is your chance to get your feelings off your chest." Gold whispers as Nadera walks back towards us.

"We are about to leave. Do you need a ride home?" I ask Nadera before I have a chance to think about it.

"Is this an invitation, Homer? Something tells me this is more than a ride home." she asks.

Gold hooks up with a girl he is close with and wants to know if we want to get something to eat. After Nadera gets the okay from her folks, we are off.

Once in the car, we talk about the test for a minute, but I have other things on my mind. I go into a sermon about how much I really appreciated her gesture before the second session. I am almost in tears telling Nadera how much she means to me and how I really want us to rekindle our relationship. We know what does not work between us. We discuss these differences to move forward. By the time we get to the restaurant, we are back in a relationship again. I want to kiss her to make it official, but I still have alcohol and weed in my system. If she detects it on me, the whole thing is off. Gold is extremely happy because he kisses the both of us when we tell him the news.

Nadera and I end up spending the rest of the day together. We decide to go to a movie, but we both need to change clothes. I am wearing some worn out shorts and a t-shirt. Nadera is in her cheerleading sweats. We go by my house so I can shower first. My mother is home from her overnight trip. While I am in my room, she inquires about what happened last night because one of our neighbors informed her about the yelling about three in the morning. I tell her the truth and my sister is furious. I quickly change the subject by telling her I have a date with Nadera and she is downstairs. My mother's mood shifts quickly as she heads downstairs to talk to her. Elise threatens me by saying she will inform my mother about my weed smoking and drinking. I really do not care because I have Nadera back.

Over the course of the next few months, our relationship is great. I drive her to school in the morning and take her home if our after-school schedules are the same. She knows deciding on a college is weighing on me.

"Homer, maybe you need to go ahead and make your college choice. Prolonging the decision is a huge burden for you."

"I am waiting on my ACT scores. Once they arrive, I promise to make my decision as soon as possible. Let me know your choices to see if, by some miracle, we land on the same campus."

"I have Middle Tennessee, Butler, UCLA, and Pepperdine on my list."

"Damn, I have Michigan, Georgia Tech, Florida State, Arizona State, Virginia Tech, and MTSU on my list."

"You are lying to me, Homer. MTSU does not have a top golf program. Whatever, just promise me you will make your decision as soon as you receive your test scores." Nadera instructs before kissing me good night.

We are such an item; we get invited to each other's family functions. We exchange Christmas gifts again. I send her flowers on Valentine's Day again. She bakes me a cake.

Unfortunately, spring is approaching, meaning our time will be limited by my golf and baseball schedule.

I receive my ACT scores. I get the twenty-four I need to get into the school at the top of my list. I score a thirty on the math portion. I want to do something special with Nadera before things start to get hectic. I plan a special date at a nice restaurant. I pull out everything. I wear a suit, have flowers waiting for her when she gets in the car, and I make a tape of all her favorite artists to listen to while we are driving.

Nadera has a special gift for me but wants to save it for after dinner.

"I got my ACT scores. Just like I promised, I made my college choice while I was in the shower before our date. I am setting up an official announcement with the press. After narrowing things down, I will attend the University of Michigan."

"Damn, Homer, why so far away? I thought you would stay closer to home."

"Why? I need to get as far away from South Memphis as I can. Michigan has everything I need. The Business school is rated in the top 10 in most surveys."

"I thought you would have tried to be close to me. Sounds to me you have thought it out thoroughly." Nadera states with sarcasm.

"What? I do not know where you are going!" I state as I ignore her sarcasm.

We change the subject and talk for hours about everything while walking beside the river. We stop a few times and kiss passionately. We also fog up the windows in the car. We decide to go back to my house for a moment. Nadera gives me my gift once we settle in on the couch. She has kept press clippings since my sophomore year in a scrapbook.

"Why are there extra pages?"

"I saved some extra pages for future clippings. I want to paste a state championship and an amateur title." Nadera sincerely expresses.

The next thing I remember is us making out on my couch. This is like us kissing at her house last year, except no one is around. Things gets very intense. She is on top of me, I am on top of her, I have her makeup all over my shirt, and we grind on each other hard.

Sex is in the air as I attempt to remove the top part of her dress. I think fear kicks in because Nadera suddenly freezes. I can tell she has allowed herself to get too worked up. She isn't ready to go beyond this step. Nadera rethinks for a moment and we try again. This time Nadera is really into the moment. Her grinding against me is more intense while on top of me. I want this be our first sexual encounter. However, I can tell she is still not ready. I pull back and offer to take her home. I drop her off and we kiss each other good night.

As soon as spring is in full swing, things start to deteriorate quickly once I get to the state tournament. Because I keep winning, I qualify for the national amateur tournament. I lose in the finals of the single match play in the state championship. I beat myself with all the missed opportunities to make birdies and settling for pars. My opponent is not a good player but is able to capitalize on my errors. The consolation prize is not too shabby. I qualify to play in the national amateur tournament in Florida. I do not have the time for Nadera like I did during the fall and winter. When I am home, it is school, golf, baseball, golf, and no time for anything in between.

One Friday, after a practice round with my uncle, Nadera calls and asks to see me immediately. We agree I will come over sometime during the evening. All Nadera wants is some time alone. I can tell she is upset by the lack of time we are spending together. While explaining how our time will be limited until golf and baseball season ends, Nadera begins to kiss me. We end up like we were on our last date. I unzip the top part of her jacket and kiss the exposed skin around her brassiere. I pull down the strap from her shoulder and begin to kiss her chest. I end up licking around her areola area once I see they are exposed.

The doorbell rings, quickly ending the session. I stay around a little longer because Silver drops by the house. I leave about 8 PM because I have a community service project in the morning and a baseball game in the afternoon. Something doesn't feel right because Nadera barely kisses me goodbye. This is odd because normally our goodbye kisses are intense.

The next morning at my community service project, the officer whose friend I supposedly mistreated when he was drunk, is giving me flack about being a taker. I let it go because my thoughts are on my game in a few hours. Plus, I do not understand what he is talking about. Once the project concludes, I am heading to my car when a group outside our organization walks up. I recognize one of the guys because we play baseball against his high school team located outside of our district.

"Hey, quit talking to that taker." A voice yells from behind us while we talk.

"What is he talking about?" I ask my friend.

"A rumor is spreading about something that happened with Nadera. Nadera told some guy you forced your way onto her, and she is thinking of filing charges." He confides as the wind escapes from my body.

He overheard all of this during the car ride to where we are gathered. I immediately think of our goodbye kiss. Is this

193

why she kissed me like that? Because we were so intense, I thought she was okay with what I was doing. The revelation of a criminal charge will ruin my scholarship. The guy giving me grief was on the phone listening because it was a three-way call. Nadera wasn't aware he was on the phone. I am too furious at this point. I know I must leave the scene before I end up committing a real crime.

Before I unlock my car, my demons and anger get the best of me. The demons advise me not to be passive on this one. I do not give them a chance to finish their advice. I go straight for this bastard. Before anyone can separate us, I have already connected two blows to the face. His followers try to assist him as the other members of the organization and the fraternity members try to break us up. We are separated for a moment when I see another opening to get some more anger out of my system. I should have been the bigger person by being passive on the issue. However, my demons and I tell this voice to go to hell as I continue to go after him again.

While being separated again, I get turned into a bad position. I am caught in a bear hug by one of the college guys as my opponent breaks free. They tie him up but the momentum of the group spills over to the guy holding me back. This forces the weight of about nine young men to push us into a concrete wall. I fall into the wall shoulder first and I immediately feel an excruciating pain. I know something is wrong when I can barely lift my shoulder. The head members of the fraternity want to discuss our actions. I disregard their request and pull off immediately heading to my baseball game.

At the game, I can barely lift my shoulder to participate in warming up my arm. One of my teammates, Deuce, who witnessed the altercation, begs for me to tell coach I am injured. I go to my regular position in left field and snag two good balls, which are good hits away from the other team in the first and fourth innings. My coach is upset by the way I am throwing the ball back to the cutoff man. Because of the injury, I cannot put any zip on the ball. I go to bat at the bottom of the fourth inning and hit a blooper to right field. I can feel the vibration of the bat up my arm to my shoulder. I steal second as the next batter hits a hard shot to left center field. The center fielder defends the ball on the first hop. I am shocked when the third base coach gives me the signal to go home. Halfway down the third base line, I hear Deuce, who is the on-deck batter, telling me to slide. The center fielder disregards the cutoff man and throws a fantastic ball to the catcher, forcing him out of the base line a bit to his left. The ball is high as the catcher makes a leaping catch to secure the ball. When he turns towards me to make the tag, we have a massive collision. This guy is every bit of six feet, five inches tall weighing about two hundred and fifteen pounds. He plays tight end on the football team. I am every bit of six feet, two inches weighing one hundred and thirty pounds.

I hear the umpire yell safe. I lay on the ground for a moment because I do not know where I am or what is going on around me. I begin to walk back to the dugout on my own when I feel my equilibrium is not balanced. I hear coach faintly yell to not let me look down at my arm. Suddenly, I begin to vomit on the field. I notice I cannot lift my right arm at all. It looks as though it is hanging lower than normal. Once the pain settles in, I fall in front of the dugout. I hear coach yell to someone to call an ambulance because my pupils are dilated.

I remember the ambulance ride being a blur and seeing my father in the emergency room. I cannot hear anything anyone is saying. I do hear when my father tells me in what appears to be a slow voice that I have a concussion and a dislocated shoulder. The good news is I do not need surgery. The bad news is I am out of service for eight weeks. Damn! I can't have a dislocated shoulder. I am headed to Florida next week.

I stay overnight in the hospital because of the concussion. My pupils being dilated cause some concern for the ER doctor. Word travels fast because the Michigan coach calls twice to find out the extent of my injuries. I am very quiet and refuse all visitors. I am upset by the events. I realize I brought all of this on myself. This is true punishment for my sins. My main concern is finding out if is there is a way to cut the eight-week recovery time down to four weeks. After the doctor talks about the physical therapy and recovery, my mother, grandfather, and I realize the best thing for me to do is to withdraw from all tournaments and events to focus on rehabbing my shoulder. I can aim for one or two events in the middle of August, but my game will need fine tuning with a lengthy layoff. After giving my mother the reassurance, I am okay with withdrawing from these tournaments, she calls my coach and private instructor to tell them my decision.

Hole 17 – Resurgence

Due to being under the influence of pain medication for my shoulder, my demons are constantly talking to me in the hospital room. Even though I like being high on the drugs, it makes the demons antagonize me even worse. The demons are annoying to the point where I request the nurse to remove the pain IV.

Brick comes to see me later in the evening. Since we are alone, I confess to him what got me in this position.

"Homer, you must learn how to control your anger. You can't be so hot headed."

"I agree. I let my emotions get the best of me."

"Don't worry about the situation with Nadera. She probably fabricated some of what happened to break up with you. Use this time to get everything in order. Reflect on everything that got you in this hospital bed. Once you pinpoint all the negativity, kick it all out so you can focus on the positive." Brick sternly states.

I am released the next day after my CAT scan reveals I do not have any damage to my head. I have the option of being home schooled for the rest of the year, but I choose to go to school because it is close to the end of the semester. The truth is, I do not want to be at home alone with my demons.

I miss the first part of the next school week to get my rehab schedule in line with my class schedule. I am at home with one of my cousins, Brick's wife, when Nadera calls during a break at school to check on me. I am glad she calls but I am short and brief with Nadera. I am still upset about hearing from someone else I attempted to force myself on her against her will.

"I can tell by your facial expression her call brightened your entire day." My cousin states while teasing me a bit.

"Yes, it did. However, it is time for me to move on from Nadera. I do not think we are ever going to make this work. Plus, I need to focus on me." I somberly confess.

Right as my cousin is leaving, Aimee stops by the house to drop off a copy of notes and assignments from our classes. I want to get out of the house because I have been bedridden for about three days. I ask her to take me to a restaurant nearby so I can eat with someone. I offer to pay since she copied all my class notes. We start off talking about our upcoming final exams.

"How are you going to take your exams with your writing shoulder in a sling?" Aimee asks while laughing.

"I will probably look a little awkward trying to hold the paper and attempting to write with my left hand. I will fail if the exams are in essay format. They will never understand my handwriting." I reply jokingly.

After some more joking and humorous conversation, I need to ask Aimee some serious questions.

"Did Nadera talk to you about what happened Friday night?"

"No, Homer. The only thing we have been discussing is the seriousness of your injury. She is worried about you being able to play golf at a high level again. What happened between you two, Homer?" "Never mind, I think I know what is going on." I interject to close the discussion.

"You must know she is seeing other people."

"This is a reality I hoped was untrue, but you confirmed my gut feeling."

"Nadera is struggling with some internal issues. Since you were not readily available, she decided to fill the void by beginning to date other guys. Another guy was over at her house before you arrived on Friday. Since Nadera's sister is working for a concert promotion company, she gets backstage passes to musical acts who come to town. Nadera is tagging along and beginning to meet some members of various groups."

"Her curiosity is probably beginning to kick in because she is attracted to these types of guys. I know Nadera has interests in being in the music industry. She probably figures someone will provide some insight on breaking into the administrative side of the business. Nadera may be a little naïve to believe these guys are taking a serious interest in her because they meet girls like her every night."

"Are you upset about this Homer?"

"No, I am not upset. I realized after this weekend I need to focus all my energy on me. Look, I am tired of talking about Nadera. What is going on in your world? I heard you had a bad breakup with the guy I warned you about. Tell me everything." I state, changing the subject because I am beginning to get upset.

"Wow! Homer, it has been a long time since a guy has asked about my feelings."

Aimee talks for a while about everything in her life. Once we make it back to my house, Aimee and I review our class notes. She helps me rub some cream on my shoulder to relieve the inflammation.

Aimee and I have always been attracted to each other, but we know our boundaries because of her friendship with Nadera. Due to both of us being vulnerable from our past relationships, the attraction almost turns into reality. As Aimee looks at me with my shirt off, we both want to engage each other. Just as we are about to kiss, we both begin to laugh. We both know this is not right. My laughter turns into tears because of the uncertainty of my future. Aimee immediately leads me to the couch, where I lay my head in her lap and cry my frustrations out. I am mostly upset about my stupidity and my feelings for Nadera. I can control my stupidity, but I cannot control my feelings for her. Aimee also cries out her frustrations. We both cry to the point where we fall asleep on the couch. After about ninety minutes, we both awake with Aimee holding me in her arms. Aimee silently gathers her things and quickly makes her way to the door.

"What's the matter, Aimee?"

"Thank you, Homer!"

"For what?" I ask, confused.

Aimee never reveals why she is thankful. She sensually kisses me on the mouth before she gets into her car. I take this moment between us as a sign. It is time to set Nadera free from my heart. If we are meant to be together, then we will meet up again when the time is right. This does not mean I am shutting her out altogether. Nadera is still my friend, and she can still lean on me for friendship and support.

I am fortunate enough to have some teachers who are sympathetic to my condition. The teachers do not know the true reason for my injury. They are under the impression I had a freak mishap during a baseball game. In my Honors classes, my biology and world history exams are multiple choice answers. I point out the answers while the teachers bubble in the scan sheet. Biology is my weakest subject. I need a high 'B' or a low 'A' on the exam to get a low 'B' grade for the year. My biology teacher helps me out a bit by lightly thumping my hand with a pencil when I give a wrong answer.

For English, our term paper we worked on for the entire year is our final exam. I can't type the last portion of my paper. Aimee offers to help me type it out, but I decline because she needs to concentrate on her final projects and tests. My aunt helps me because she is an English whiz and has superior typing skills. The paper is complete before spring break, but I must type out the conclusion, bibliography page, and the table of contents.

My topic is the influence of Muhammad Ali during the civil rights era. I read countless books about the man, look at videos of his early fights, and study his interview techniques. My aunt's opinion on my paper is positive. The points I cover are thoroughly researched and well expressed. My English teacher has a different opinion because I end up with a 'C' on the paper, causing me to get a high 'C' for the year in the class. She is an older Caucasian lady who probably disapproves of the subject matter because of the media's depiction of Ali during this time in history.

My calculus teacher is creative by giving me an oral exam because I cannot write out the answers to show my work. I have the same questions as the other students, but I must verbally explain the answers and concepts. I stumble at first because I know the answers, but I am having problems articulating my responses. Each question is like a tricky clutch putt to win a match. After I approach the remaining questions with this thought process, I do well on the exam. I impress my teacher with my knowledge of the subject matter. I get a low 'B' on the exam giving me a 'B' for the year. This is a victory for me because this is the hardest class ever. This teacher pushed our mental capacity to the limit daily. I am mentally and physically exhausted after the exam. The English grade is the only blemish on my report card for the year.

The school year is over, meaning it is time for me to focus on rehabbing my shoulder. My grandparents come down for my sister's graduation. I need my grandfather during this time. He helps by talking to me for the entire week. I tell him everything, but he does not scold me because of my actions. He just explains to me to learn from my mistakes.

I face a board review for the fight on the day of my injury with my organization. The guy I fought, and I are put in front of a panel to explain our actions. We discover the root cause of the problem being the night I mistreated his friend for slapping my sister. He confesses to intentionally exaggerating the Nadera incident to get revenge for his friend. The panel asks him what he would have done if his friend slapped his sister. In conclusion, the panel strips him of his officer duties. I am placed on probation. We are both still in good standing for the party on graduation night. In a one-on-one conversation after the panel hearing, we both apologize for what happened and agree to move forward without any future retaliation. Since the guy admits to exaggerating Nadera's statement about a sexual assault, I never confront her about this incident.

I am miserable at the party because it is packed tight. I cannot mingle through the crowd because any brush against my shoulder hurts like crazy. One of the guys in our organization is the DJ for the party so I stand next to him on stage the entire night. A miserable situation turns into something positive because I can see the entire dance floor and motion to the girls I want to pursue. I do well with the amount of phone numbers I collect. Leslie comes to the party with her squadron of good-looking girls. We try to touch base for a while because I haven't seen her since I started dating

Nadera again in the fall. Leslie is looking good! It is too loud to get into a good conversation. We agree to meet up later to talk.

Thankfully, a fight breaks out, ending the party early. I recently purchased a pager and ask her to beep me once she is settled. I am sweating profusely because I am in a shirt and tie. I need to go change clothes and shower if I am going back out later tonight.

I am tolerating the pain in my shoulder. The ER doctor prescribed me pain pills, but I do not like the way they make me feel. Plus, the demons I am already fighting seem to surface more frequently while I am on the medication.

I arrive home to a packed house of relatives. I get cleaned up and play around with a few cousins before I get Leslie's page. Leslie is winging it home alone. Leslie's mom's flight into Memphis is canceled, pushing her arrival time back to early in the morning. Leslie wants to come to my house because I am right by the airport. I explain my house is overly packed. We instead agree to go to a midnight movie. I lie to my mother, telling her I will stay at Silver's house because I cannot take the crowd. My mom does not give up my bed because of my injury. I willingly let someone else have my bed for the night and I let my mother know I am feeling fine. I am lying because I am in pain and starting to get a little depressed when I think about what may happen down the road. She agrees to let me go but I must be back early because she needs my car so everyone will have transportation for the day my mother has planned. My mother questions me about not having a bag. I'm wearing some basketball shorts, a regular t-shirt, and a pair of running shoes without any socks. If I look as though I am going on a date, she will not buy into my plan. I explain to her I will sleep in what I have on, wear it home, and change clothes in the morning.

By the time I arrive at Leslie's house, she changes her mind about the movie. Leslie is tired from a long day. I agree and we go straight to her room to call it a night. We alter our normal sleeping position due to my shoulder. While getting everything situated, I accidentally brush against Leslie's breasts.

Apparently, she is aroused by this light touch because she begins to kiss me. I feel weird at first because I haven't kissed anyone except for Nadera for the last eight months. In the back of my mind, I think I need to stop and have Leslie sign a waiver stating she is a willing participant. I do not want to hear any rumors of a possible rape charge in my future.

My last sexual encounter was a little over a year ago and I am feeling a little uneasy. The perturbed feeling dissipates when she starts kissing me again and straddles me while I am on my back. The feeling from her mouth before she places me inside her dispels all my uneasiness. I think about what I told myself. It is time to start thinking about me. The demons also emerge to tell me to just lay back and enjoy the moment.

After enjoying our sexual experience, we both lay silent, taking in the moment.

"Damn, Homer! I was tense and frustrated from my final exams, breaking up with my boyfriend, and trying to narrow down college choices. You took all the stress away. I can tell you were a bit tense also. You did wonders for someone with one arm." Leslie states as she walks across the room to open a window.

I am in a spell for a moment looking at her body in its most natural form. It arouses me again.

"Yes, I was. I also went through a bad breakup. Worrying about rehabbing my shoulder has me frustrated a bit. You realize we did not use protection." I state as Leslie pulls out her stash of weed from under her bed.

"No need to worry, Homer. I am on the pill."

"Okay, but how many partners have you had in the past?" I ask nonchalantly while beginning to smoke some of her stash.

I can tell Leslie has already been hitting the stash before I arrive.

"You know I am not that kind of girl, Homer." Leslie confesses as she seductively takes the weed from my lips to begin kissing me again.

This leads to another episode. I am reluctant to participate because I do not believe what Leslie is telling me, thanks to Brick's advice on trusting women. However, my demons surface once again. They use the sin of lust to overpower my rational thinking. It does not take long for my body to give into what Leslie is offering. This time, I take control. I please her with my mouth before having her lay on her stomach. This time, I do not forget to use a condom. My delivery is rough due to my frustrations being at their peak. The harsher I deliver to Leslie, the more she enjoys the encounter. She reaches her climax for the second time before I can. Due to both episodes being highly intense, we are both sound asleep within ten minutes.

Both episodes take place in less than forty-five minutes. I wake up just before dawn and begin to stare out the window for a while. Even though Leslie's and I experience is great, I know this is not love for me. As with my other encounters, it is just sex. I want love. As a kid who is about to turn seventeen, yes, I want love and not just a feeling. For some odd reason, I begin to think about Nadera while finishing the weed Leslie and I started smoking earlier.

"Look over your shoulder at this girl lying under the covers. If I were you, I would end this fantasy and go back to see if you can get lucky a third time." My demons express.

205

I agree with them and climb back into bed. The attempt is a success and I have sex with Leslie for the third time. This time, it is more sensual and passionate. While driving home, I realize I have some major mental issues to address.

After a couple of weeks, I begin physical therapy. The rehab process takes its toll on me during every visit. I push myself to the limit during each session thinking this will speed up the recovery time. I cry during the exercises because they are so intense and excruciating. Even though the pain is intense, I refuse to take the pain medications. I have exercises to do at home, but I end up doing putting drills with my left hand since my right shoulder is to stay stable. I work my way up to using both hands by training my right shoulder to stay stable during putts. Aimee accompanies me to my rehab sessions on her off days or before she goes to work. She is deeply concerned about my recovery because she knows how much golf means to me. Aimee pushes me harder than the therapist and does not show me any sympathy when I cry.

For eight weeks, I repeat this daily routine. I hate being alone every afternoon after rehab. I fill the void by spending a lot of time at Tee's house after therapy sessions. Tee is staying home during the summer while his parents are at work. I reopen my recruiting because the Michigan coach ends up taking another coaching job on the west coast. I would have kept my commitment, but the new coach never calls to check on me to see how my recovery is progressing. Since I am injured, I am not receiving many calls from the nation's top schools. The coach who was trying to recruit me to help him build an up-and-coming program keeps a watchful eye on me by calling like clockwork every Wednesday. I feel the coach is genuine with his concern because he does not use this time to give me a recruiting pitch. He keeps giving me words of wisdom to help me get through my physical therapy sessions.

Nadera calls a few times a week to check on my progress. If she does not talk to me, she is discreetly talking to my mother to get an update. I feel her concern is authentic and our conversations are strictly on a camaraderie level. If Nadera initiates us, attempting to try restarting our relationship again, I don't think I will jump at the chance. I am not putting myself out there again so I can end up hurt, but it is nice to know I still have her shoulder to lean on if I need it.

My eight weeks are over! I receive medical clearance from my therapist and my primary care physician to start swinging my clubs. I can't wait to get back on the driving range and start playing practice rounds. There is only one problem; I do not have any money to pay for the range or golf fees at a course. My sister is on her way to college in a few weeks, so I know my mother and father are stretched financially. I am embarrassed to ask them for money, so I go to the most unlikely source. I page Brute to setup a financial arrangement.

I set up a business and repayment plan for Brute to review. I make my way to one of Brute's stash houses for a meeting. I am not greeted well because Brute has moved up in the ranks with new personnel in his entourage. They are looking at me as though I am an undercover NARC because of my Caucasian appearance. Fortunately, Tike appears and kills the tension. He walks me in the backroom where Brute is counting a mountain of money.

"Hey, Homey, I need to frisk you before you enter." one of Brute's security people demands to make sure I am not wired or armed.

"Don't worry, Homer. It's business, nothing personal. You can't trust anyone these days." Brute sternly states.

After I check out clean, Brute's demeanor quickly changes.

"Where have you been Homer? What is so urgent for you page me 911?" Brute asks as he greets me with a hug.

"I am in a bad spot, Brute. I need some money to get my golf game back on track. I need new equipment, clothes, and money to practice. I intend on paying you back. He is a repayment plan I put together."

His crew chuckles while I am describing the repayment plan I printed.

"Hey. Chill out. This is serious to Homer. You idiots can learn something from this." Brute scolds his heavily armed crew.

"The cost for everything I need is listed…."

"Tike! Make sure Homer gets five stacks before he leaves." Brute yells while cutting me off.

"Brute, I only need about six hundred. I cannot pay back five thousand."

"Hey, I am investing in your future. Don't worry. You will pay me back soon enough. You are going places with this sport of yours Homer. Listen to me. Get away from here. I guarantee when you come back you will make a difference around here." Brute seriously expresses.

Tike hands me an envelope containing fifty-one-hundred-dollar bills.

"Brute, I know a way he can pay us back and make a few extra dollars." Tike states as he hands me the money.

Tike describes what is needed. It will require me to make a few runs for Brute around the neighborhood. Even though I feel a little uneasy about doing this job, I know I must because I may not get out of this house alive if I decline. Even though I know this is wrong, I agree and leave as quickly as possible.

I immediately go to the driving range close to my house. I spend about five hours hitting balls until the manager closes the property. Even though I am hitting the ball well, I am not hitting the ball like I was before my injury. It is mid-summer and I purposely start my practice rounds in the afternoon heat to get my body back in shape. Training your mind to focus in hot humid weather when your body is depleted of fluids is not an easy task. Since I have been laid up for eight weeks, I am not in shape like I need to be to get through a full round carrying my bag. The manager at Pine Hill suggests I use a pull cart before I start carrying the bag on my shoulder.

In the summer heat on a weekday, I have the course to myself. I carry a few sandwiches in my bag and freeze a gallon of water in a milk jug every night to stay hydrated. Two elderly ladies who work the grill and concessions at the golf course notice how hard I am working every day. They are kind enough to make sure I eat a full lunch and rest a bit in the air-conditioned clubhouse just so I can catch a break from the brutal heat.

My first few practice rounds are horrible. I play three balls. I am hitting the balls clean but I am not accurate. After my practice rounds on the course, I go to the driving range and hit more bad shots. This is driving me completely berserk. I talk Aimee into meeting me at the driving range to film my swing so I can analyze it on tape with my aunt's video recorder. After filming, Aimee and I have lunch to talk. She catches me up on what I have ignoring over the summer.

"Please remember the promise you made to look after yourself. To me, it seems you are breaking this promise by hibernating over the last eight weeks. You need to get out and have a little fun." Aimee expresses.

"Right now, my focus is on getting my game back on track."

After reviewing some video with Brick and my uncle, they tell me I need to relax. Gold pages me so we can get out and run the streets for a while later in the evening. I haven't seen Gold, Silver, or Bronze during the summer because we all have our own things brewing.

On a muggy Sunday evening, I pick up Gold, Silver, Aimee, and Lisa. We have been invited to a summer barbeque by a friend who lives on the other side of town in a well-established neighborhood. We all have a good time during the long ride to her house. It feels good to laugh because this is something I have not done all summer.

Silver and I always make fun of each other. We quickly get back to teasing as soon as we get on the expressway. I have to stop teasing because our laughter is causing me to lose focus on the road. We discuss our upcoming plans for our senior year of high school and which colleges we are considering. Aimee and Lisa are close with all of us. They do not mind us talking about girls in their presence. Well, Aimee does not mind Gold and Silver discussing other girls.

We all talk about who we are dating over the summer. When they get to me, I am silent. Gold and Aimee know who has my heart, but silently understand I do not want to discuss Nadera in Silver's presence.

"Homer, you will probably meet a girl today." Lisa states.

"He always meets someone wherever we go." Aimee says with cynicism.

"He meets them but does not follow through." Silver adds.

"I believe Homer has homosexual tendencies!" Gold states as we all burst into laughter.

Gold knows I am struggling with the feelings I have for Nadera. Therefore, he coins the phrase 'homosexual tendencies' as a cover up.

"Maybe the person he is looking for is sitting next to him in the front seat." Lisa adds, referring to Aimee.

"Hold it, guys! Homer and I are good close friends. I care for him deeply, but that is the extent of our relationship."

The message Aimee gets across to the passengers in the back seat is a smoke screen. She surreptitiously caresses my hand to let me know how she truly feels. I am silent during the conversation because the only thing I care for right now is my golf game.

When we arrive, it is like a mini party. The scene is full of cheerleaders and girls from the dance team. The ratio of men to women is to our advantage until some members of the local university basketball team arrive. These guys are treated like royalty because they are the closest thing we have to a professional franchise. Their teams are always nationally ranked, and all the games are sellouts.

Crystal is at the party, and we strike up a conversation. Leslie is here as well. She is upset at me because I have not called to talk since our sexual episode. Everyone asks me about my shoulder and my progress. I am getting a little tired of talking about it until a member of the basketball team asks about my injury.

Tony is a local basketball legend who is a for sure lottery pick in the NBA. Brick and I attended some of his high school games. This guy is awesome. He pulls me to the side to discuss recruiting, grades, and injuries. Tony had to sit out his freshman year because of a pulled abdominal muscle from a freak accident off the basketball court. He has an awesome sophomore year and there is a lot of hype on his upcoming junior year with the supporting cast on the team.

"I have been reading up on you because I am a fan of the game. I felt bad when I read about the injury to your shoulder. I know you are disappointed about missing the national amateur tournament. Hey, take it from someone who had a freak accident. You need to keep moving forward."

"Man, I am struggling to get my game back on track."

"Trust me, it will come. Don't force it. Be patient and you will be better than you were before the injury. Take your time with your recruiting. You will know when to make the right decision. Now, let's forget all the serious talk and go over there and get on some of these girls." Tony adds as we both laugh.

This conversation has a real impact on me.

Once the afternoon dies down, Silver suggests we head to a new mall to check out the scene. It seems like everyone at the party joins us on our journey. Gold, Silver, and I have a field day checking out all the summer bunnies walking around. We do not discriminate. It does not matter if they are black, white, Hispanic, or Arabic. If they are good looking, we are spitting game for a phone number.

When the mall closes, we head to the Crystal Palace roller-skating rink to hang out in the parking lot for a while. This is a good hang out spot. Most of the people who show up are only on the scene to show off their cars as they cruise through the parking lot. I am hugged up with Aimee on the trunk of my car when Brute, Tike, and Red walk up.

I haven't seen Red in a while. We end up talking for a long time. Red is only in town until Labor Day. All three are high on something. I drink a beer with them, but I reject anything else because I am driving.

Looking as lovely as ever, Free walks up to give me a big hug. Her body has filled out into a more developed, curvaceous figure. We exchange phone numbers and agree to go out sometime soon. A little tension begins to grow in the parking lot with some rival gang members, so we decide to pack up shop and leave before something pops off.

I drop Lisa and Silver off first. I drop Aimee off next. She pleads with me to give her a call to let her know I made it home while walking to her front door.

"I really enjoyed spending time with you today. I could have hugged you in the parking lot all night.," I whisper, which leads to Aimee giving me a sensual kiss on the cheek.

Gold and I decide to ride through the Southgate Shopping center and downtown to see what is happening. After talking about the girls, we have seen and met, Gold and I get into a deep discussion.

"Homer, Free is looking good. Please follow up on that. What is up with you and Aimee? I noticed the way she kissed you."

"Gold, I love Aimee. She has been by my side all summer. She accompanied me to almost all my rehab sessions. However, we will not take our relationship beyond friendship."

"Is this because of Nadera?"

"Yes!"

"Alright, Homer, what is truly bothering you? I can tell you had a good time tonight, but I sense something is troubling you."

"I must be wearing cologne named tension because this is all I have been hearing lately. I don't know what to feel anymore. I feel numb to everything going on around me. After the injury, I just feel deflated. The only satisfaction I want is to have my game come back to me so I can compete where I left off. I don't enjoy anything except for when I have my clubs in my hand. I had sex with Leslie and didn't enjoy it."

"WHAT! Why?" Gold asks in shock.

"It was just a temporary fix to escape what I was feeling at the time. Don't get it twisted. It felt good but I wanted to feel some sort of love."

"Well, damn! At least you felt something!" Gold responds while laughing. "Well, Homer, tell me if this is true: you are still in love with Nadera."

"No doubt, Gold! I thought about her right after I had sex with Leslie. I think about this girl constantly. When I leave Al's Golfhaven, I want to make a right out of the parking lot to her house around the corner. I still talk to her as a friend. She calls occasionally to see how my golf game is progressing. I love the fact that no matter what is going on, we always connect just to make sure everything is going okay. If she pages me right now and says she wants to try again, I probably will be trying again before we hang up the phone. On the flip side, I just can't open my heart again for her to crush it. I have too much on the line right now. I don't want anything to ruin my mindset." I state with sincerity.

"That's good and all, Homer, but you can't continue to fill these voids with temporary fixes. I am not saying to turn down sex from a girl, but you need to make sure you at least feel something for them, so you don't string them along. And if your dumbass is thinking about Nadera after sex, then it's obvious where you need to be. With her! Both of you are so freaking stubborn. Think about it. It is about to be our senior year. What about the homecoming dance and the prom? It is only fitting you two go together."

"Damn! The prom is like ten months away. Let me get through the golf season first. To be real Gold, I love her, but

I am afraid of her. If it's meant to be then we will be together again." I state somberly.

We go back and forth on the subject for a little while longer while driving.

We finish riding around at about two in the morning. I take the long route home because I am not tired and want to ride a little while longer. Leslie pages me a few times. I stop at a gas station to return her call. She wants me to come to her house. I agree to make sure we clear up any hard feelings between us. I figure the ride will help me sort some things out in my mind. I am blasting and cruising to a homemade tape I made of Prince slow jams.

Once I make it to Leslie's house, it does not take long to clear the air. The reason we are not talking is mainly due to hectic schedules and focusing on our own individual goals. Before we realize what we were doing, we are having another sexual experience in her den. It is not too rough or too slow, it is just right. It is a session fulfilling our emotional needs along with satisfying our raging teenage hormones.

Afterwards, we talk for a moment to discuss being in a relationship. I am hesitant at first because I am heading into my senior year and golf season starts in a few weeks. I agree because there is not a reason for me not to be in a relationship with Leslie. I like everything about her. Leslie is smart, I know she genuinely cares for me, she is absolutely gorgeous, and she does not care about my racial makeup. I figure it is probably a good thing we are at separate schools. This way, I can focus on school and sports without the distraction of trying to maintain a relationship with a girl at my school.

We fall asleep on the couch and my natural body clock wakes me up at about five o'clock. It is Monday morning and I need to get home before my mother wakes up to go to work. Leslie understands, which makes me feel exceptional. She makes me something to eat before I depart. Prince got me to Leslie's house but the Isley Brother's 'Voyage to Atlantis' and 'Summer Breeze' takes me home. The melody of the songs provides a calm ride for an early Monday morning. I make it home about five forty-five.

I know my mother is going to give me a hard time. I am fortunate my mother is knocked out cold from being out partying herself. When she wakes up for a moment to run to the restroom, I know she is about to explode in anger.

"Are you up early to go play a round of golf?" my mother asks.

"Of course! What other reason would I be up this early?" I answer, lying.

Right then, I knew this night was destined to happen.

I fulfill my promise to Aimee by letting her know I made it home. I take a power nap before getting ready to play golf with Brick at seven thirty. This night is what I needed to get my mentality back on track.

Hole 18 – Closing the Round

Things start to change over the next few weeks. I finally get my game on track, learn how to balance my time, and I am starting to have fun. Time is going by so fast because of all the senior activities we must complete before school even starts. Even though I am in a relationship with Leslie, I am spending most of my time with Aimee. We are still struggling with taking our relationship beyond friendship, but we act like we are together in public. I am still following Brick's advice on piecing a girl together.

Free and I begin to date. Crystal and I are seeing more of each other. Crystal and Aimee are the ones I can hang out and talk to without any expectations. Leslie is the show piece for ego reasons. I take her to events with large gatherings like the mall, concerts, and parties. In the public's eye, people know Leslie and I are a couple.

Free and I use each other for physical pleasure only. Free is a liberated spirit who is open about sexual relations. She is what you want your wife to be like when it comes to pleasing a husband. Free is a lady in public and an all-out maniac behind closed doors. She does not care how, when, where, or what she must do in order to make sure you are pleased. Free's only request is for me to put in the same effort in her she bestows. Free makes it crystal clear she is not a jump off type of girl. Free will not allow you to treat her below her standards. This is not a problem for me because I have known Free since elementary school.

Even though I care a little bit for all of them, they cannot become Nadera because she is the complete package. We both do not take Gold's advice to try to give our relationship another try. Nadera's sister introduces her to an older guy and they instantly mesh, establishing a long relationship. Am I upset? Yes, but I understand. Our curiosity is leading us down separate and different pathways. My feeling is if Nadera is happy, I am pleased.

I play in some local end-of-summer golf tournaments. I win all of them, but it is against subpar competition. I am not pleased with my play. I use these tournaments to get the feeling of playing competitive again. During the last tournament, before the start of the school year, I figure out what is lacking in my game. I am trying to force my game back instead of letting the game come back to me naturally as Tony advised me to do.

I ride this momentum into five rounds of golf a week and hitting the practice range early in the morning and on weekends. The putting stroke I developed during my rehab stint is beginning to pay off with great results. I am going to the tougher courses in my area to expand my game. I push myself by playing from the championship tees and attempting difficult shots from various lines on the courses.

Some of these courses are expensive but the money I got from Brute is covering everything. After I buy some new clubs, my confidence is high going into golf season. My high school coach begs me to stop playing because he does not want me to wear myself out before the start of the new season.

My senior year finally begins, and it is great from the start. My sister is away at college, so I do not have to negotiate sharing the car. My mom is spending a lot of time out of town because of work. I only need four classes to graduate but must take five because of state requirements. I am getting out of school an hour early every day. Overall, I am a happy individual. A group of us, including Aimee, leave school to get something to eat and return before the rest of the school is dismissed for the day. I can go home or straight to the range, but I use this time to keep my work and life balance in order. The socializing keeps me from over analyzing and focusing too much on my golf game. I spend most of my free time with Gold and Silver. I start pursuing some of the girls I previously rejected, including a sophomore I have my eye on. I am not too focused on my schoolwork because I have the GPA and the test scores to go to any school of my choice. At this point, all I need is to have a good golf season and I can have my pick of any college.

After our first two matches, I am in high demand again. I am in the zone. I break some course records with my individual scores. The team is doing very well, feeding off my momentum. We beat the team who won the city championship and placed runner up in the state tournament by a huge margin. I am having some long days by leaving the house by seven and not returning until well after dark. After a match or practice, I go to the driving range by my house to get in more practice. The Michigan coach finally calls to see if I am honoring my verbal commitment. I voice my concerns about not hearing from him while rehabilitating my shoulder. After our call, I publicly state I have officially reopened my recruiting. I should have kept this to myself because this opens the flood gates because universities all over the U.S. are calling once again. Flashbacks of the stress from last year surfaces. I hold off visiting schools again until after the season is over.

This year, the state's athletic governing board decides to have the team and individual state tournaments at the same time due to budget reasons. In order to make sure we have enough daylight hours to complete the year end tournament, they push the season forward to start the first week of school. School starts in early August, and we are allowed fourteen matches during the season. By the time Labor Day weekend arrives, we are twelve matches into the season. We win eleven of those twelve matchups. Our only loss is due to a bad outing from the entire team. Due to playing on an unfamiliar course, we cannot get it going against our rival high school where Leslie attends. She rubs it in every time she gets a chance. We have a tough schedule due to coach pairing in matches against private schools where the competition is fierce. Unlike my teammates, I am in shape for it by playing five times a week and walking in the extreme July heat with my golf bag. August in Memphis is ruthless due to the heat. I am beginning to change colors from being in the sun. Gold teases me by telling me, I still haven't got my shade right yet.

The rankings for the state are posted before the city championship. Our school is ranked in the top five of our classified districts. Before the city championship tournament, Coach announces I am in the running for golfer of the year in our region. I can't wait to tell my mother and grandfather.

"Grandpa, you must come down for the tournament. I am ranked in the top five in the state and in the top twenty nationally. Can you come, please? I am begging."

"I do not think your grandfather is up to traveling, Homer. He is not feeling well." My mother states from another phone in the house.

"What do you mean? He was down here a few months ago for Elise's graduation. He looked fine and well."

"We are both proud of you, Homer. You have worked very hard to get to this point but..."

"But what guys? I am not ten years old anymore. What is it?"

"You are right, Homer. You are not ten anymore. I always promised I would never lie to you about anything. I cannot come due to a kidney procedure because of my diabetes." My grandfather states sincerely.

"I cannot attend either, Homer. I am flying to Virginia for the procedure." My mother interjects.

"No worries, guys. Even though I want you to be here with me, I understand. I'll make you a promise. I am going to get you a city and state trophy."

"That's my boy! I know you will!" My grandfather replies proudly.

On the first day of the city championship, I am a little nervous because it is the same day my grandfather is having his procedure. Since the course we are playing is fairly easy, I post a decent score. I should have posted a better score, but my mind is on my grandfather. As always, Brick, my aunt, uncle, and cousins are there for support. My paternal grandmother shows up late once I complete my first match.

"Your mother called. There were some complications with your grandfather's surgery. He pulled through the procedure, but his recovery will take a little longer." My grandmother tells me while holding my hand.

"How did you get to the course? You normally do not drive after three o'clock."

As soon as I finish asking her the question, I see my father in the background.

"I wanted to make sure you are okay. Plus, I have never seen you play." My grandmother replies.

I can tell my father does not want to be a distraction. He deliberately stays incognito until I am finished. Since the tournament is held on a city course, I think he uses this as an excuse to see me play. We do not say much to each other. However, I notice him in the background on every hole, observing my round during my second match. I want to tell him I am glad he is here. I am glad someone told me about my grandfather because I do not think I would have played the way I played if I did not know if he was alright or not.

After my play for the day is complete, I kiss my grandmother on the forehead.

"Thanks, Grandma! I am glad you told me about the procedure so I could concentrate."

"No problem, Homer. I know your mother is out of town. Make sure you are at my house before tomorrow's morning round so I can put something in your stomach."

"I can manage. Tomorrow's round is early in the morning. I will have to be at your house about five -thirty to make it to the course by six forty-five."

"Boy, are you arguing with me? Don't make me have you look for a switch to straighten you out in front of all these people."

"Yes, ma'am. I will be there first thing in the morning." I agree, knowing it will be a long day.

I eat dinner at my aunt's house before going home and resting up. I cannot do my homework because I am still worried about my grandfather and tomorrow's round. I cannot talk to him on the phone because he is under sedation. It feels odd not talking to him about my round. I normally describe every round to him after I settled in from playing. It is funny how God works because the phone rings on my line. It is a voice I have not heard in a while.

Nadera is calling to check on me.

"You sound troubled. What is the problem?"

222

"It is hard to describe over the phone." I reply.

"Why don't you come by my house so you can describe what is bothering you."

"Are you sure?" I ask to make sure I hear her correctly

"Yes, boy! I will meet you in the driveway."

I do not shower from playing but I change into a clean t-shirt before leaving. When I arrive, Nadera is waiting for me on her driveway, still in her practice clothes from cheerleading. This girl is still stunning even without any makeup and wearing a sweat suit. She is absolutely gorgeous.

"Your mother told me everything going on with your grandfather. I know you talk to him after every round. Talk to me like you do to him." Nadera expresses.

Nadera sits patiently on the trunk of my car as I spill out everything over the next thirty minutes.

"Are you nervous about tomorrow?"

"I am pretty confident I will do well because my game is in sync right now."

"You need to watch your confidence, Homer! It can cause you to make bad decisions. Think it out all the way through before executing the shot." Nadera bluntly states to me.

"Wow, Coach!" I reply as we both begin to laugh.

The laughter makes us open up to each other a little bit more as we discuss colleges and obstacles bogging us down.

"Have you decided on a new school yet?'

"No, I think I have it narrowed down but I have to visit one more school again before committing."

"Is one of them Butler?"

"Is that where you have decided to go?"

"Yes, I got my scholarship papers in the mail today."

"Wow! Indy, huh! Should I inquire about their golf program? Just kidding, I know they have a good marketing program. Getting a scholarship is damn good. I am proud of you." I respond to Nadera's news while giving her a hug.

After we hug, Nadera jumps right into her main concern.

"Homer, are you in a relationship? I hear you and Leslie are doing well." Nadera slyly asks while rolling her eyes.

"You should know I can't manage a relationship during the fall and spring." I reply as she begins to laugh.

I am not about to tell her about how I piece together a girlfriend. I definitely will not mention Aimee.

"Nadera, are you happy?" I ask, intentionally leaving out asking if she is in a relationship.

"Yes!" Nadera answers proudly.

"That is all I need to hear!"

We talk a little while longer about everything except for our feelings. This is a good thing because we would probably end up arguing. Nadera gives me something I really need tonight. Nadera makes love to me. Not love in the physical form, but she makes love to my mind by providing her friendship and support.

"I am still waiting to cut out a city and state championship, Homer!" Nadera yells with her back to me while she walks towards her house.

"This is why I love you!" I say to myself as I get into my car.

"I know you do, Homer. I love you too!" Nadera states from the carport.

She must have felt the vibe from my heart because I barely said this over a whisper.

We play the team round at another course in the morning, and we will start the individual match play rounds in the afternoon. I make sure I am at my grandmother's house bright and early. Today is going to be a long day because I must get up early, play the team rounds for the city championship, run to school to take an Advanced Algebra test, head back to the course for the start of the individual rounds, and be at a football game against our rival at seven. Whew!

We breeze through the morning round to capture the team city championship. I take my Advanced Algebra test and flunk it with ease. I know the work, but I cannot focus like I need to make a good grade. We attend a pep rally for the football team where the principal announces we won the city championship. We barely get a few handclaps. I get a few cheers because I am somewhat known throughout the school. My teammates are a little shunned, but they must understand the Caucasian population at the school is dwindling. Most of the African American students do not care about the sport.

I bump into Nadera before I leave to go back to the course. She whispers, reiterating what she told me last night. She noticeably kisses me on my cheek in front of Aimee. I can tell Aimee is furious. Nadera's kiss is the motivation I need because I beat my first two opponents on the front nine in each round. I never make the turn to the back nine in both matches. I easily qualify for the semifinal round at my home course at Pine Hill on Saturday.

After doing some interviews with the local paper, I leave for the football game. Since I am already late, I do not change clothes. It does not matter because I am going to be outside anyway. When I get to the game, I need to grab something from the concession stand because I am starving. I bump into Gold who is waiting to hear about the results. During a quick break from their cheerleading duties, Nadera and Aimee want to know the same thing. Nadera is happy to hear about my results, but her boyfriend is in attendance. She makes our conversation seem casual, using Aimee to make it look unnoticeable to him. Aimee pulls me away from the crowd to give me a congratulatory hug and kiss behind the bleachers.

Leslie is at the game because we are playing her school. As usual, she is traveling with a platoon of good-looking girls. People are used to seeing us out, so it is not a big surprise as we hug and kiss when we greet each other. Leslie is looking superior as always. Most people outside my circle think we are a couple, but everyone in my inner circle knows the truth.

"You may want to keep your distance. I smell bad from being on the course all day."

"Whatever, Homer, you know I do not care about that, boy!" Leslie replies as she playfully punches me as I speak to everyone in her group.

"I'm not going to monopolize your time since you are with your friends. Do you want to hook up after the game?" I ask Leslie.

"I do Homer, but I drove tonight, and I have about five people in my car." Leslie replies before whispering in my ear. "We need some alone time, Homer, if you know what I mean. I have been missing you."

"I need it too, Leslie. We can work it out afterwards. My mother is out of town. Just page me when you get done." I whisper back before we give each other a departing kiss.

I have a few friends on the football team so I want to see how they are playing. Since we are winning the game with ease, I begin to focus my attention to the gathering of females in the crowd. I am finally able to link up with the sophomore I've had my eye on for weeks, but I did not have the time to talk to at school. We hit it off well and exchange information. Silver is joking with me because I am playing the field with

Leslie in the crowd. Leslie is not paying attention to what I am doing because she is too wrapped up mingling through the massive crowd.

A group of us decide to hook up after the game at my house until we figure out our next move for the evening. I bump into Crystal and her friends, letting them know to meet us at the house. I tell Aimee and Lisa about our plans. I invite Nadera even though I know she will not show up.

Aimee and I leave a little early to link up with my cousin so she can buy me a couple quarts of beer. Plus, I need to take a shower and straighten up a bit before people arrive. We also make a quick stop at Aimee's house so she can pick up some fresh clothes.

Aimee shocks me by joining me in the shower because she also wants to clean up from cheerleading during the game. I am fully engaged in the moment after Aimee allows me to view her fully exposed. Damn, I was not expecting this today. We test our friendship boundaries while drying off. We begin to kiss ferociously. I am not sure what has gotten into Aimee, but she is the aggressor. We are centimeters away from voiding the friendship boundary when I stop for a moment to get a condom. It literally hurts me when Aimee wants to stop.

While getting dressed, Aimee lets her feelings about me known. I explain I want more than friendship, especially after this episode of affection. I am erect to the point where it hurts. Once we get dressed and straighten up a bit, we take a moment to share a blunt to try to calm down our hormones.

Gold, Silver, Bronze, and Lisa arrive, and they immediately want to play some cards. Lisa goes straight to the record collection to listen to some music. After about an hour, Crystal and her friends show up. About twenty minutes after they arrive, a few other friends in our circle arrive. Right before my eyes, a major party is developing.

Leslie pages me and she brings her circle of friends. We have a card game in the kitchen and a craps game starts on the living room table once some of the players from the football and basketball team arrive. The alcohol is in the backyard as well as serving as the designated smoking area. It turns into a good outing except for one major problem—I have to be at the golf course at seven. I am not worried about getting some rest because I will be up away thinking about my game.

I will not allow people upstairs, but this does not stop Silver. Silver has a girl in Elise's room. Crystal and I are on the basketball court talking with a group of folks when Leslie flags me to come to the back gate. She is leaving and wants to meet at her house once everyone leaves. Things turn sour when I explain I must be at the course early and Pine Hill is located a short distance from my house. My reply must have angered Leslie because she suddenly storms off. There is too much going on around me to run after her. I figure she will be okay. Just as we have done in the past, we will get to the bottom of what is bothering her after I finish playing tomorrow.

Upon returning to the backyard, I notice Aimee and her boyfriend having a deep discussion about something. I never met this guy, but he somehow finds his way to the party. I look for her about fifteen minutes later, but she is nowhere in sight. Lisa and Crystal inform me she left with her boyfriend.

About forty-five minutes later, the party starts to dwindle. Gold, Bronze, Lisa, Crystal, and a few others stay around a little while longer to chat and goof off. Lisa and Bronze help me get the house back in order. Silver is still upstairs doing his thing. Bronze is getting a kick out of listening through the door. We do not get a look at the girl he has in my sister's room. While we are all in the den after cleaning up, Silver rushes her through the front door and rushes back in to take a shower.

We all make our way to the front porch because everyone is about to disperse. The time is approaching two thirty as we start to engage in another group conversation when Crystal pulls me to the side.

"Homer, do you want to go out tomorrow night?"

"Sure, I have not made any definite plans." I respond.

Out the corner of my eye, I see a car pull up and quickly realize it is Leslie's after the light's cutoff. Gold announces to the group it is time to roll out because I have some business to handle.

After everyone departs, Leslie tries to explain her actions. As we go in the house heading to my room, I tell her not to worry about it. Leslie makes sure I am not tense for my match play games in a few hours by having hard, intense relations. She does not know I am already worked up from my interaction with Aimee. We both laugh afterwards because we agree it is our best session to date.

"I can accompany you for your first match tomorrow, but I go to work at twelve at the clothing store. I know you will make it to the championship round, Homer. I hate I am going to miss it." Leslie states while I get dressed to go practice some putts downstairs.

"I understand. You have your priorities. Thank you for tonight. I have a lot on my mind. You took away my worries for a while." I state to Leslie while I give her a long sensual kiss.

When I arrive downstairs, Silver is on the couch eating while watching videos on TV.

"You and Leslie woke me up." Silver laughs.

"Man, who was the girl you had in Elise's room all night?"

"I am taking her identity and the experience to the grave." Silver replies while laughing harder.

Once I pull out my practice green, Silver wants to bet to see who can make the most putts. Silver is a pretty good golfer but never pursues the sport because it is unpopular amongst young African American men. We are playing twenty-five cents per putt made. After about an hour, he only owes me about a dollar.

"Homer, you need to get some rest for tomorrow." Leslie states as she makes her way downstairs.

"You are right. I can still salvage a power nap."

"I thought I heard you down here with someone. I am glad I didn't come downstairs naked." Leslie states as we all burst into laughter.

We head upstairs to rest up. Silver wants me to drop him off at home before heading to the golf course. Leslie and I do not get much sleep due to trying to recreate the moment we just shared a short time ago. We are both tired, so we ended up making slow love to each other.

I am awakened by the phone ringing. My mother is calling to wish me luck and teasing me, wondering if I have a girl in my room.

"Yes!" I state joking.

"Is it Nadera?"

"It is only Silver and I in the house. He is asleep in Elise's room."

I have yet to introduce Leslie to my mother.

I am glad she calls because she is in the Eastern time zone. If she hadn't called, I would have overslept. I am finally able to talk to my grandfather. He is still a little weary from the medications from his procedure. Even though I can barely understand what he is saying, I take his mumbling as telling me good luck. My grandmother reiterates his thoughts by telling me to knock whoever I am playing on their hind parts.

I still have about ninety minutes before I need to leave. The phone wakes Leslie up. She jumps in the shower while I am talking to my folks. Based on the experience with Aimee a few hours earlier, I jump in with her to try to recreate the moment. I give Leslie credit for doing everything she can to keep me focused on the tasks I have in front of me. She administers some forbidden activities in the shower I only have seen in adult movies. She cooks breakfast for me and Silver, irons my shorts and shirt, makes sure I have some snacks to put in my bag, and drives me to the golf course.

After we drop off Silver, she talks to me about everything outside of golf to prevent me from going into mental overload. When a song comes on the radio, I immediately feel terrible because I am wishing Leslie is Nadera right now. I think about the conversation Gold and I had a few weeks back. I need to stop using Leslie and the others as fill-ins to compensate for the void I am feeling in my heart. Leslie is beautiful and smart. The only reason I will not commit to her is because I am in love with someone else.

"I really appreciate your company and everything you are doing right now. Thank you for coming back last night. Maybe it is time for us to turn the page on this relationship and try to move it forward a bit. I know we committed to each other over the summer, but I want to know if the way things are now between us is working for you. I know I cannot give you all my time and energy. I think what I am giving to this relationship is unfair to you. I do not want to drive you to someone else to fill the void." I state to Leslie in a debonair mode.

"I was hoping to have this conversation last night. This is why I got mad when you said you wouldn't come by my house. I care about you deeply…"

I freeze when she starts this sentence.

"However, I do not want us to get too wrapped in each other because we are at different schools. I know you are getting approached by girls because I noticed how they were coming on to you at the football game last night. I may meet someone else and want to go out with them. You may want to do the same as well. I just think we will make things difficult if we define ourselves to being in a relationship. I like the way we are spontaneous and how things turned out last night without planning. Everything just flows when we are together, and I want to keep it this way. I think the quality of our love making will diminish if we categorize ourselves as a steady girlfriend and boyfriend scenario. I hope I didn't let you down by telling you this." Leslie states.

"Oh, I am glad I brought it up for discussion. I think I can work with the way we are now."

I am jumping up and down inside with joy. I do not have a reason to feel bad anymore. I can keep my date with Crystal without feeling remorse.

I arrive at the course and go straight into my warmup routine. I am happy to see my aunt, uncle, Brick, and my grandmother. I introduce Leslie to them, and I am relieved when she tells my aunt and grandmother we are real close friends. My father shows up and asks me how I am feeling. I let him know I am good and ready for whatever is in store for the day. Gold and Bronze show up and they both tease me before the match about being a true 'white dude' for playing the game. Gold walks with me to the first tee to talk to me one-on-one about Leslie. I give him the full details of our conversation on the way to the course. Gold is just as relieved as I am about the relationship.

The wind is coming in random gusts, but it is not concerning enough for me to rethink my strategy. I find out my first opponent is a sophomore named Bruce from a private school who is loaded with potential. Bruce reminds me of myself due to his racial makeup. The only difference is Bruce comes from a well to do family. His mother is an attorney, and his father is a well-known U.S. Senator. Just like myself, his parents are divorced, and he has a rocky relationship with his father. I played against him in baseball. He will play in the Majors one day if he sticks with the game. I am trying to read him to pick up any vibes of doubt.

Once I shake his hand, I know I have him by the way Bruce grasps my hand and the look in his eyes. The kid is too timid because of fear but not because of his lack of ability. I end up beating him by six holes. This young kid has some serious game but is not at a point where he trusts his skills. I shake hands with Bruce and his mother. I express to him he will play for the championship again before he gets out of high school. All he needs is more experience under his belt.

As I turn back towards my bag, I shake hands with all my folks following me for the round. After talking with them, I look down at my shirt and shorts to realize I am drenched in sweat. Even my socks are wet from the perspiration.

"Homer, you need to keep up the intensity you showed in this match. If you show the same intensity this afternoon, you will beat whoever you play." My grandmother states while pulling me down to her eye level to give me a kiss on the forehead.

"She is right, Homer. Your intensity was off the chain." Gold adds.

"Man, I am so thirsty right now." I tell Gold while looking in my bag to get some of the snacks Leslie prepared, but they are all gone.

"Homer, you knocked those snacks out between holes six and ten." Leslie tells me.

Between not sleeping last night and sweating profusely, I do not think I can make the walk back to the clubhouse. Fortunately, Coach is in a golf cart. He gives me and all the women a ride back to the clubhouse.

I give an interview to the local newspaper's sport reporter who followed the match. I mostly give praise to my opponent's potential and then dart to the parking lot. Leslie has to leave so she can make it to work at twelve. I have her drop me off at the house so I can change clothes and get my car before the championship match at three. After I find out it is only about ten thirty, I stop rushing because I have plenty of time. We shower together again, have sex again, then shower again, and Leslie gives me an alcohol rub to ease the tension around my neck and shoulders.

Before I get in the shower the second time, I realize I am not hydrated because of the color of my urine. I must fix this immediately. After getting out of the shower, I jump on the scale and notice I lost about six pounds of fluids. Leslie quickly cuts me up an apple and banana with a glass of water to start the rehydration process. I have a bottle of Gatorade and immediately gulp it down.

"Make sure you eat before going back to the course." Leslie commands.

"I am going over my aunt's house who lives right by the course before going back this afternoon."

"I will page you later to find out the results. Even though I know you will win." Leslie states before giving me a long, sensual goodbye kiss.

I make it to my aunt's house at about one and she prepares a light lunch for everyone. After eating, I go to the living room couch to take a short power nap because I am exhausted. She wakes me up about two fifteen so I can get back to the course to warm up. The clubhouse is a short walk from my aunt's backyard. Instead of driving, I walk out the back fence and stroll to the practice area. I left my clubs in the manager's office so I would not have to tote them around. I take a thermos from my aunt's house and consume all the water before I make it back to the clubhouse. I hang out in the air conditioning in a chair by the restroom because I need to make sure I am hydrated before the match starts. I am attempting to fill my thermos when the marshal advises me, there are water coolers setup every five holes and at the turn to the back nine. They were there during the first match, but I did not notice them. Coach rushes into the bathroom telling me they need me for the coin toss and stating of the rules. I quickly relieve myself and head to the first tee.

While walking to the first tee, I see a familiar face talking to my grandmother. I think it is a mirage from being dehydrated, hungover, and sleepy but the person is real. Silver and Gold distract me for a moment by sneaking up from behind and jumping on my back.

"Is that who I think it is Gold?"

"Yes, Sir Homer! Your heart has arrived."

There are a few other friends who arrive to support me, but I brush them off to get over to Nadera.

"I can't believe you are here." I tell Nadera.

"I came with Silver. You know I had to be here to support you, plus I have yet to see you play. Hopefully you are not all hype." Nadera responds softly.

Damn! I get weak when I get a whiff of her signature perfume.

"Now, go get my press clipping!" Nadera whispers in my ear.

It absolutely drives me crazy. With Nadera here for support, I know something magical is about to happen.

I am surprised my championship opponent is one of my teammates named Kyle. We exchange some friendly jabs on the practice putting green. Kyle introduces me to his parents, and I introduce him to my folks. I win the coin toss and elect to tee off first. Bronze cracks a few jokes about my shorts drawing a bunch of laughs while I am getting a couple of golf balls out of my bag. I quickly ignore the laughs as I slowly drift into the zone I found a few years back in Texas.

Once I tee up my ball and look down the fairway towards the green, I can hear some voices on the side, but I completely hush them in my mind. I always know when I am in the zone because I only hear the birds, the sound of the leaves crackling as the wind goes through the trees, and when I see the morning dew on the grass in detail as the sun evaporates the moisture. Being in the zone makes the ball looks as though it is a softball while teed up. My club feels like it is an extension of my arms growing from my body when I grip it correctly in the palm of my hands. I can shape my shots with pinpoint accuracy before I swing the club. The zone is also a place my demons cannot penetrate. There are no distractions, inner voices, or second guessing. I trust myself completely when I am engulfed in this mindset. The zone is where I need to be, and I am fully swallowed by it.

I hit a beauty down the right side of the fairway. Kyle hits his ball in the dead center of the fairway but is about thirty yards short of mine. Even though we finish the first hole tied, I can tell he has come to play. We are all square after six holes when things start to turn around in my favor. The seventh hole at Pine Hill is rated the number one handicap on the course. Kyle and I have played this course numerous times. We both know going to the right on this hole is trouble. If you hit a good drive to the left, the approach shot is a bit easier to an elevated green using a seven or eight iron. There is a nasty hillside bunker on the left side of the green, which comes into play from this angle. The right side is nothing but trouble because it is lined by tall pine trees and unhittable patches of thick, rough grass. It is the kind of grass where you can easily lose a ball because it will sink in the bowels of the roots never to be seen again. There is a silver lining if you are skilled enough to a play a draw to skim the tree line and land on the down slope of the fairway about two hundred and fifty yards down. If the shot is hit perfect, the ball will roll a few extra yards to the right of the fairway, leaving a short crisp wedge to the green. It also takes the deep hillside bunker out of play on the approach shot. This shot is extremely risky but is worth the reward if executed correctly. If the execution is flawed, it is a for sure bogey or worse.

Kyle takes the safe route by going down the left side. I am about to do the same until I feel the summer breeze come across from right to left. I hold onto my three iron for the longest time until I hear my uncle say go for it. Even though I cannot see him because I am so focused, I nod my head in the direction of his voice to let him know I hear his instructions. I grab my driver and shape the shot in my head before swinging the club. As soon as I go into my backswing, I feel the wind adjust from east to west to northwest in a moment's time. When I contact the ball, I get the greatest feeling in golf. I feel nothing. The ball takes off directly to the trees just as I shaped the beginning of the shot in my mind. I hear Brick and my uncle telling the ball to turn as it gets closer to the trees. The club does its part by assisting the ball's slight turn to the left. It is now up to the wind for the shot to have flawless execution. The wind is a little late as the ball taunts the tree line. Just as the shot is about to look like a failure, the wind kicks in to assist the ball's draw. As soon as I notice the shot is shaping out as envisioned, I reach down to pick up my tee because I do not need to see the ball land. I know it is perfect.

"You are a bastard! You have been holding that shot back all season." Kyle states jokingly.

"I got lucky because the conditions turned out right to execute the shot." I reply, laughing.

The wind, being in the zone, my friends and family support, and especially Nadera being here make the conditions perfect. I hear some cheers and slap my uncle's hand while walking to my ball.

Kyle hits his approach shot short of the green into the twelve-foot-deep hillside bunker. The next shot is impossible because there is little green to work with out of the sand. Because of my tee shot, I take the deep bunkers out of play. I can hit a soft wedge to within eleven feet of the hole. Knowing my teammate's game, I know he will not get aggressive and hit the ball out of the bunker towards the green. The only way out is to advance the ball backwards and then hit a chip shot onto the green.

I am shocked when Kyle goes for the green from the bunker. The ball comes out clean and hits the flag stick. Unfortunately, the ball hits the stick at an angle. This causes the ball to shoot out to the right on the fringe of the green. I can tell Kyle is frustrated about executing a perfect shot with negative results. Kyle lingers on this shot while executing his next shot because the outcome is horrible. The ball ends up on the other side of the green, causing a lengthy putt for par. All I need is to sink this putt to get a lead. Playing Silver for money on putts a few hours ago pays off. I carry out the putt for a birdie to lead the match.

I completely kill my drive off the tee on the next hole, which is a par five. Kyle is still holding on to the bunker shot, causing him to hit a bad slice off the tee into the thick rough separating the fairway from the previous hole. After this shot, he is pretty much mentally eliminated from the match. By the time we get to the thirteenth hole, I am up five holes with six holes left to play. All I need is to halve the hole and I am the Memphis City and Shelby County champion.

The thirteenth hole is a short par three with a creek in front of the green from a slightly elevated tee area. The back of the green is surrounded by three hidden bunkers. The right side is lined with trees and the left side is a wide-open patch of thick rough. The only shot on this hole is to hit the green. The pin placement is on the front side of the green close to the creek. Since there is a lot of green to work with, I hit a nine iron with three fourths power to not go over the green and hopefully generate a little spin on the ball so it can hit dead center and come back towards the hole. I have been working on this shot since I lost to Eric in Dallas.

I hit it with the right amount of power. In error, I hit the ball too high, causing it to come to a dead stop once it hits the green. Kyle tees his ball and attempts his shot to the hole. He hits the flagstick again causing his ball to ricochet into the creek. Once he gets his ball onto the green, Kyle concedes the hole, giving me the win.

"Kyle, you just got some tough breaks." I whisper while giving him a hug.

"The match was over when you hit your tee shot on number seven. Homer, that was the best shot I have ever witnessed." Kyle exclaims.

Before celebrating with my friends and family, I walk with my arm around Kyle's shoulder to his parents and shake their hands as well. Coach gives both of us a huge bear hug. It is the first time Coach has a city champion and the runner up. Brick and my uncle both give me big hugs. My aunt and grandmother hug and kiss me on the cheek. My father tells me he is proud. Gold, Silver, Bronze, and the others in attendance jump on me like I won the Super Bowl.

"I got your press clipping!" I state to Nadera while giving her a hug.

I hold on to her a little longer than needed. It feels perfect to be in her arms after my accomplishment.

"Ugh! You are getting me wet, boy!" Nadera exclaims. I am drenching wet again from the heat and humidity. "I have never seen you so focused and concentrated. You amazed me today. I thought I knew you, but I learned something more about you today." Nadera adds.

As I let go of her from our hug, she notices my tears and wipes them away. I begin to cry because she knows my struggles and my path to get to this point.

"They don't need to see you crying." Nadera articulates while holding back tears herself.

The same reporter I spoke with earlier in the day comes up and asks me a few questions.

"How do you feel about this victory?" the reporter asks.

"Honestly, I need to go to the bathroom." I reply as we both laugh. He allows me to conduct the interview afterwards.

After a brief celebration at my aunt's house, I go home to clean up and change clothes. Gold, Silver, Bronze, and another friend are playing cards at my kitchen table. Before getting into our normal Saturday night routine, I call my mother to tell her the news. Due to being full of adrenaline, I forget I have not been to sleep. Brute and Tike hear about my win and stop by to celebrate by smoking the biggest blunt. Brute also slides me about three thousand dollars for the accomplishment. I make sure no strings are attached before accepting.

My cousin stops by to participate, along with bringing a few beers. I phone Leslie at work, and she wants to celebrate. We have already made plans to go to the mall where she works. Leslie shares her congratulations while we are in the food court during one of her breaks. Leslie wants to go out once she gets off work, but I have already made plans with Crystal. I let Bronze drive my car to drop me at Crystal's house so she can drive because I am worn out and a little high. I let him use my car so I will not drive under the influence. I advise him I will page him once we return from the movies.

Crystal and I make it to the movies, but I fall asleep in the theater. I am so tired when we get back to her house; I fall asleep on her couch while we are watching television. Her mom wakes us up when she notices us asleep on the sofa. She does not freak out or anything. Crystal's mom gives me a blanket and a hard time about sleeping on her couch while she makes breakfast. Her mom knows I am tired from partying all night Friday and playing in the heat on Saturday. Crystal and her mom have a relationship where they share everything. She tells me breakfast is her gift to me for winning the city title. This is the exclamation point to conclude the weekend.

I must put the city title behind me to focus on the state title. I get my progress report and it shows I am failing Advanced Algebra for the six weeks. According to the bylaws to play sports in the state, you must pass five classes with a 'D' or better to participate in athletics. I am only taking five classes so failing one is out of the question. I talk to my teacher, Ms. Rogers. After shuffling some points around, she gives me enough to get a 'D' for the reporting period. The only reason she cuts me some slack is because I participate in class. She knows I can do the work. As soon as golf season is over, I must stay after school and make up the extra points through one-on-one tutoring. I know this is a close call, so I do not mess around with her class or the coursework for the remainder of the school year.

The next weekend, I am off to the state tournament. Middle Tennessee State is about thirty miles from the tournament location. My high school coach allows me to visit the campus with my mother and aunt.

My aunt takes education seriously and assists my mother to make sure I am making the right decision on selecting a school. She grills the administrators and golf coach about the curriculum. The school looks different from my last visit. The coach impresses me with the direction he wants to take the program.

"I see you are impressed, Homer. Are you ready to sign now?" The golf coach asks.

"In all honesty, sir, I am reluctant because I am not sure you will be around for my full tenure at the school. You are an up-and-coming coach; bigger programs will court you to lead their team in a couple of years. If I commit to attend MTSU, you are the main reason for me wanting to come to the university. I appreciate you checking on me when I was injured. You gave me some great words of encouragement that got me over mentally. I do not want to go through a coaching change in three years. I want to go through my playing years with you." I express to the coach with sincerity.

"I understand. I am here for the long haul, Homer. By you signing with MTSU, it will boost the program immediately. I want you to help me build the program to a powerhouse. You can help me recruit other players in the coming years. We can do this together."

"Wow! Coach, I want to give you a commitment today. However, I still need to weigh my options." I express.

I think the coach feels good about the visit due to the extent of our conversation. I feel good about the visit because none of the coaches I have spoken with have given me a recruiting pitch like this gentleman. I am exuberated someone feels I can help build something special. Feeling needed or special is an emotion I have been longing to experience.

The state tournament does not go as planned. We come in third for the team title. I am the runner up for the individual title. The match is close, but my opponent gets relief from a lie, which normally does not allow reprieve for a player. I contest the ruling with the match official. The match official does not find where my opponent has done anything illegal based on the wording in the rule book. I request the head official for the tournament to weigh in on the incident. He agrees with me the wording in the rule book is nebulous. After some conferencing on the course, they cannot come to an agreement on the wording in the rule book. They allow my opponent the relief from the lie where his ball is located.

The relief allows my opponent to hit an awesome approach shot on the seventeenth hole about five feet from the cup. I miss my birdie putt to halve the hole. I also miss a birdie putt on number eighteen, which would have sent the match into extra holes. My opponent makes his par to win the title.

"You are all hype half breed." my opponent whispers as we shake hands afterwards.

I laugh as I walk off the green. I am not mad at my opponent. I am more upset at the official because after doing an interview with the local news crew, it is discovered the officials made the wrong call. "How do you feel about the ruling?" A local Memphis reporter asks after the misruling is revealed.

"This is the way things line up sometimes. Am I upset? Yes, because I worked hard to get to this point. If the ruling does not affect the outcome, then coming in second is not an issue. The ruling does influence the outcome, so now I am paying the price for someone else's error. I will note this down as a learning experience and I know what to do going forward."

"What will you do?" The reporter asks.

"I know I need to start out by being more aggressive, scoring on the holes I need to score, and taking more chances. If I win, I win. If I lose, I lose. At least I have control over the outcome and know who to blame. I can't let anyone else control my fate. I will sleep soundly tonight but my opponent will forever know his title win is flawed." I reply, angrily. My opponent's father hears my comment and aggressively starts berating me. He charges to the area where I am standing. I am shocked when he is stopped in his tracks.

"Talk to me. Don't talk to him." My mother states, jumping in front of this man.

I overhear them exchange words. My opponent's father calls me a sore loser and how my mother needs to teach me some manners. I couldn't hear what my mother said to this man, but he quickly rushed away in the opposite direction.

"What did she say to him?" I ask my grandfather.

"Your mother just let him know she had some fireworks in her purse if he got any closer to you."

The state athletic commission issues a statement attempting to rectify the situation. My mother discovers the official of our match is close friends with my opponent's father. His previous opponents during the tournament also complain to the commission because it seems ironic this one guy officiated all my opponent's matches. Each of these matches involved numerous favorable rulings. The official admits his wrongdoing but there is nothing in the state athletic commission bylaws to do anything to my opponent because there is no proof of any wrongdoing on his behalf. I have a feeling if it was revealed my father had any association with an official, I would have been stripped of the championship and blacklisted by the colleges on my list.

After my mother and I talk to the committee, we ask them to not pursue any further action because I am comfortable with the public apology. I figure my opponent will suffer more than I will afterwards. After a long discussion with my grandfather and mother, I advise the committee they need something in place to prevent this from happening in the future. Besides, second place does have its privileges. I qualify for the regional amateur tournament this spring and a few other tournaments against top players from around the country. The way I am playing, I know I have a chance to do some amazing things. When interviewed by a reporter from my opponent's hometown, I purposely emphasize this gentleman will forever be punished because he will look at his trophy and know it was purchased. This is payback for the comment he made after our match was over.

The Clubhouse – Finishing this Round

I am glad golf season is over for a few months. I can chill out for a while and enjoy my remaining high school days. I get a chance to rest up and spend a lot of time partying with my friends. I attend lavish parties at country clubs. Rich white men, who are members of these prestigious establishments, ask me to take their daughters to different venues. These guys do not have a clue about me. Because of my appearance, they think I am of Caucasian persuasion. They think because I play golf, I am from a well to do family with a privileged upbringing. They take my ethnic accent as being from the Louisiana bayou area. I also listen to some of their terrible racist jokes and comments. I play the part very well by laughing along. I get back at them by taking advantage of these rich men footing the bill for my tuxedo or suit and paying for the entire evening. Most of these fathers figure their daughters can get in on the ground floor. It will be a feather in their cap if I end up marrying one of their daughters if I become a professional golfer.

Due to not being able to control my sin for lust and revenge, I take advantage of their daughters. They give me pleasure whenever and however I want, and they are good at it. Bronze gets a kick out a sneaking into some of the rich, white girl houses with me if they have a friend over. Fortunately, I do not have to worry about running into these girls outside my circle because they all attend private schools. I do not understand why these girls are so vengeful against their folks because they have everything they can possibly want in life. Nice homes, maids and butlers, their own brand-new cars, credit cards, and free reign to do whatever they please. This is the type of environment I envisioned as a child in elementary school. I use them to my advantage by having them buy me clothes and pay for our dates. One girl lets me use her credit card frequently to gas up my car. Their fathers are members of some elite country clubs and pay my greer fees when I ask to play a round. Some even give me money on the side to try to influence me to attend their alma maters.

I am still seeing Leslie and escort her to her school's homecoming dance. I connect with the sophomore I have been eyeing. She turns out to be pretty cool. I develop some feelings for her, but I do not pursue anything major because we are at different points in our lives. Leslie is mad when I do not ask her to my school's homecoming dance because I take the sophomore to the game and dance. I escort Aimee in the homecoming court because she is running for homecoming queen. Nadera is also running. I am a little thrown off when she does not ask me to escort her during the game. I thought we connected again during the golf tournament a few weeks' back, but I guess I was mistaken.

I am doing what I am good at regarding having a girlfriend, which is piecing one together. Now, there are more pieces to the puzzle. Aimee is the only one I feel I have a connection. We still cannot figure out how to break the barrier to take our relationship beyond friendship. I spend time with Aimee when I want some quality time away from home.

As the months go by, my behavior towards some of these girls is ridiculous. I forget names and dates I schedule because I am going out of town on weekends visiting schools. Some of the schools recruiting tactics are amazing. They set out a lot of things to convince you to come to the university. They make sure a good-looking girl escorts you for the weekend. I believe some are professional call girls because some of the guides set out more than just tours.

I know I must make some changes when I throw another party at my house. I am expecting Aimee to attend but she does not show due to reconnecting with her on and off again boyfriend. I really wanted to spend all my time with her. Out of disappointment, I have sex with the sophomore I have been dating and with Leslie later after the party when she shows up unexpected. This stuff is getting old and is not fun anymore.

The deadline is approaching for me to make my college choice. After a short debate with my mother, I am ready to decide. I call the coach at the school I choose. I ask him to fax the paperwork to my mom's office. Due to being so excited, the coach comes to Memphis to hand deliver the documentation, watches me sign the paperwork, and takes it straight from my living room to the school's administrative office upon returning to campus. I advise the coach I will not announce my decision until after all documents are final and I receive an acceptance letter. Once the letter arrives, I setup a news conference at my mother's law firm. When I make my announcement, I pull a Middle Tennessee hat from under the table and place it on my head.

"Homer, why did you choose MTSU over some of the top programs in the country?" A local TV reporter asks.

"The MTSU coach was in constant contact with me during my injury, we are on the same page as to where he wants to take the program, and I feel I am the igniter to take the program to the next level."

"What about the rumors about recruiting violations?" The same reporter asks.

"Some of the schools on Homer's list did their best to persuade him away from MTSU. Some even leaked some false information to the NCAA about inappropriate recruiting tactics. I feel confident his name and school will quickly be cleared due to insufficient evidence. I ask you to please respect his decision. The location is accessible to all our family and friends who have supported Homer throughout his young career." My mother answers confidently.

She is right because a statement is issued a few weeks later by the NCAA clearing my name. The only thing I am guilty of is taking money from Brute. I am slammed by the media for picking MTSU. They report I am afraid of top competition.

With this decision behind me, I completely let loose until graduation. My friendship with Gold, Silver, and Bronze is at an all-time high. We are beginning to sound like smart young men making important decisions about our futures. Even though things are smooth and fun, the world reminds us how quick it can turn from bright to dark in only a moment.

On a crisp winter January evening, Gold, Silver, Bronze, and myself decide to hang out right after school. Our school is playing our rival team in basketball later in the evening. We just decide to goof off and spend time as old friends. We drive to the mall when Silver remembers he talked to a few girls from our school during fifth period. They are doing the same as us, just passing time and hanging out before the game.

When we leave the mall, Silver needs me to take him home to change shirts because it got dirty when a small kid accidentally spilled soda on his white shirt. The mall is a good drive back to South Memphis. I am driving and decide to avoid the expressway due to rush hour traffic. We all do not mind the ride will take about thirty minutes longer because we are not in a rush. We are in my father's custom van, making the ride comforting. It wouldn't have mattered if we were in a cramped Beetle. We are too busy laughing from funny insults and teasing between close friends.

Instantly, the mood changes when police lights are visible from behind the van. Instead of the officer coming to the driver's side to advise me of why I am being pulled over, vivid instructions are given over the intercom to show my hands. All passengers are asked to slowly exit the vehicle with their backs turned and hands up. I am asked to turn off the vehicle and drop the keys on the ground. I want to protest the instructions. My mother instructed me on what to do if I was ever pulled over. Since I cannot talk to the officer, we all agree to comply with the instructions.

Gold, Silver, and Bronze are cuffed and forcefully pushed to sit on the curb. I am not cuffed but I am placed in the back of the police car.

"Whose van is this?"

"My father's." I reply.

"If it is your father's, why is the address different from what is showing on your license?"

"My parents are divorced. I live on Prairie View and my father lives on Prairie Park in a different area of town. I don't understand the questions because we both share the same name. He is senior and I am junior."

"Shut up, punk! I am asking the questions. Are there any weapons in the van? Any drugs?"

"No, sir!"

"Why is a white kid running with a bunch of niggers in this part of town?"

"These are my friends from school. I also live in the area about ten…"

"Only answer the question I give you. If we find something in this van, we are locking all four of you up for the weekend."

I decide to just follow his instructions. I sit in the back of the car while they search the van. Watching what the police are doing is frightening but we are all getting angry. They go through everything in the vehicle, even the tapes we are listening to via the stereo. Bronze is almost shot when he reaches into his jacket once he is uncuffed to advise the officer he is carrying a pencil. Thankfully, an officer with his night stick already in hand intervenes before the gun is pulled. The officer places the tip of the stick to his chest and asks him to watch his hands. Through all the questions and harassment, no one still hasn't told me why we were pulled over.

After about an hour, we are uncuffed and released.

"Sir, am I getting a ticket?"

"We pulled you over because the vehicle fit the description of a crime in the area. You are lucky I am having a good day because I could have taken you bastards to jail."

"It would have been four less fuckers to worry about on Friday night." Another officer interjects.

"Do yourself a favor and pick some friends who look like you. Have a good evening!" The officer states while returning my license.

The ride to Silver's house is completely silent. No one says a word while we are sitting in the van waiting on Silver to change shirts.

"What the fuck just happened?" I softly state.

"And they want to know why 'Fuck the police' is a popular song!" Gold yells.

This sparks Bronze to start rapping the song at the top of his lungs. This broke the melancholy, anger, and frustration.

Silver returns to the van and all three are repeating the lyrics at the top of their lungs while I am driving to the game. By the time we reach the gym, the melancholy is gone but the anger and frustration with the police is branded into us for the rest of our lives. The only crime committed was DWB: Driving While Black.

Prom time is approaching, and I end up going to about three or four different ones. I am only concerned about my prom, and I want to go with someone to make the night special. I make plans with Leslie, but she is not the one I want to take. I want to go with Nadera. I pick up the phone to call her one night, but I chicken out. We have not spoken to each other in months. I am also afraid of the rejection.

Leslie and I get into a horrible argument. The outcome of the verbal altercation leaves me without a date. This is the last time I have any contact with Leslie until after I am married, and we connect on Facebook.

Crystal and I make plans to go but she changes her mind at the last minute and goes with a guy she just met and supposedly falls in love. I am telling Aimee in music class about my troubles. She tries to persuade me to ask one of the girls from the private schools to the prom. I don't want to be bothered with one of them.

"Look, Homer. I will be the only person left to ask if you do not do something immediately."

"You mean you do not have a date? What about the old guy you are dating?"

"I haven't dated him since the night of your last party. I have been waiting for something to fall into place."

"I have been waiting on some things also. However, I am fooling myself thinking it will ever happen. You think if I would have asked Nadera, she would have gone with me?" I ask somberly.

"No, Homer! Hell no! She is in love. Plus, I told her about my feelings for you." Aimee answers.

"How did she react?"

"She acted okay about it, but I was told she was upset because she feels you were off limits to me due to our friendship. You know both of you are going to the same school?"

"Middle Tennessee? I thought she was going to Butler."

"No, she got her scholarship papers a few days ago. Her mother did not feel comfortable with her being so far away from home. After some intense arguing and negotiating a car out of the deal, she decided to stay in state."

I immediately get quiet. Is this fate or some sort of torture? Will I have to endure her meeting and dating different guys? Should I call her to talk about this coincidence?

"Well, that is it for me. I can't continue to follow this dream. It is like reaching for the full moon that looks reachable over the horizon, but you know you can't grab it because the moon is a million miles away. What about you, Aimee? Who are you waiting to ask you to go?"

"You, Homer!"

"You mean, you want to go with me? What about being friends and not letting anyone know how we feel about each other?"

"I can't continue letting this hinder me from who I want. Plus, I think people are noticing how we interact."

"Aimee, will you go to the prom with me?" I ask with a huge satisfying grin.

"Yes, Homer. A hundred times over. Yes."

In my wildest dreams, I never envisioned Aimee and me at the prom. We have a great time at dinner. I take her to an upscale five-star restaurant thanks to Brute giving me money for the prom. I bump into him at the corner store close to my house and he slides me a thousand dollars. I still have barely spent the money he has given me in the past. I decide to drive my mother's car instead of renting a limousine.

My heart melts when I pick Aimee up because she looks astonishing in her dress. Our conversation in the car and at dinner is incredible. We talk about everything from college to our favorite cartoon characters.

I know what Aimee is worried about this evening and I am also bothered as well. When we arrive to the prom, we take a few pictures and talk to a few couples in the lobby. Due to the bright lights from the camera, Aimee needs to freshen up her makeup before going into the dance. I sit in the doorway, awaiting her return to scope out the crowd. I eventually see Nadera dancing with her date. Once I see the look of happiness on her face, I smile also. Aimee sees I am staring at them when she meets back up with me at the entryway. I sense she is a little uncomfortable.

"You look amazing!" I state to Aimee to change the mood.

"Are you sure you're ready to go in?"

My demons' surface to tell me to forget about Nadera and truly focus on Aimee. I am torturing myself thinking we will work this thing out between us. Once I concentrate my focus solely on Aimee, I end up having a great time.

Aimee and I stay out to about four in the morning. We jump from afterset to afterset until I take her home. An unexpected twist happens when we arrive at Aimee's house. We finally remove the friendship barrier preventing us from expressing our true feelings towards each other. A good night kiss at the front door ignites a passionate loving making session in the back room of her home. The experience is great because we do not hold back anything. The episode is the perfect ending to our prom night.

I am in Aimee's kitchen in my tuxedo shirt and pants playing with her dog at the table when her mother enters. Aimee is in her room changing clothes; well, putting on her clothes from our occurrence. She is not upset about us being out all night. Her mother thought she heard me leave a little while ago. She makes us breakfast. We decide to eat on the front porch to catch the red-orange sky because the sun is up.

"I really enjoyed our prom night, Homer. I had a marvelous time."

"No, thank you, Aimee! Last night was amazing. I am a little tired so I probably should head home."

"What do have planned for the rest of the weekend?"

"Just playing or practicing golf. I do not have anything planned. Hopefully I can spend some more time with you."

"Can you go somewhere this afternoon about six?"

"Sure, do you want me to pick you up?"

"No, I will pick you up," Aimee responds.

This outing turns into another outing. By the time we graduate a few weeks later, we are candidly dating exclusively. Believe it or not, I am not piecing a girl together this time. I am solely seeing Aimee. She understands when I am away playing in tournaments. When I am home, we spend every available moment we can together.

I am doing well in my tournaments. I win the regional amateur tournament, which qualifies me for the national tournament. I knock out the kid I played in the state championship in the second round. I intentionally beat him by seven holes. I am invited to play in the local professional tournament as an amateur through an exemption. Aimee walks the course with my grandfather. Aimee watches me fall on my face during the opening round. She is clapping the loudest when I storm back in the second round to make the cut for weekend play. Since I am an amateur, I cannot get paid.

"Homer, go ahead and go for broke because you do not have anything to lose. You have already proved the critics wrong by qualifying," Aimee advises me at breakfast the morning of the third round.

"Damn, Aimee, you have a point. I can go ahead and play like it is practice. I can take risks without worrying about losing anything."

I end up finishing tenth for the tournament. I could have finished higher and possibly qualified for the American Championship if it wasn't for my play during the first round of the tournament. I did gain some valuable professional experience and advice from some of the tour players. A top ten finish as an amateur creates some buzz on the national level but I am hoping my success solidifies my exit out of my current surroundings.

I have some downtime for the next few weeks before going to Florida for another tournament. I pay back my debt to Brute by doing a few runs. I run some packages to a few housing projects. I am pulled over before delivering a package during my last run. Since I am a white-looking young man in a high crime black neighborhood, the cops immediately sense something is suspicious. A white and black officer use me doing a rolling stop at a stop sign as a justifiable cause to search my car. While cuffing me, they slam my face on the hot hood of the running police car. They listen to the tapes I have in the console. When they get to the trunk, I know I am in deep trouble. They go through my backpack and find the package I am to deliver. I quickly realize I just ruined my future.

"You can come clean now because you are in deep shit if this is what we think it is." The rude black officer explains to me.

Due to thinking I am already in deep shit, I explain to the officer I am delivering a package to a friend. The black officer starts a graphic sermon about what to expect when I am locked up with the other criminals in juvenile detention. Once he pulls my license and recognizes my last name, the officer really gets vulgar.

"I went to school with your daddy. You light skin niggers think you rule the world. I hated your daddy then and I hate him now. You are no better than us dark skin niggers. I am going to make sure you are somebody's bitch when I lock you up tonight. You can kiss your golf future goodbye." The black officer rudely whispers to me.

The more he talks, the angrier I become. During these years, I never felt I am better than anyone because of my skin complexion. I always felt inferior. This ignorance of dark vs light is a malignant tumor haunting our race.

The officer is still talking nonsense when the white officer comes over to where we are and states to let me go. The black officer looks confused as the white officer shows him what is wrapped in the package. It is about eight video game cartridges taped together to look like a brick of drugs. They bust the cartridges open but nothing illegal is inside. The black officer is furious and begins to comb my car looking for anything illegal. I almost lose my bodily fluids when he finds the money. I know he is about to put it in his pockets.

"I should plant something in the car. This punk needs to learn a lesson." The black officer states to the white officer loudly.

"We have nothing significant to charge him with. I don't want to waste the next few hours typing out a report for a minor traffic violation. I don't want to explain what justification we had to search the trunk." The white officer states as faint gunshots are heard.

"But we are keeping the money? It is a nice payday. Plus, I would love to hear his explanation as to how he is in possession of so much dough!"

"We will have to explain this, too, if we don't charge him with anything. Unless we run him in for…"

"*Shots fired! Shots fired! 10-999! Officer needs assistance! 10-999! ALL UNITS WITHIN THE VINCITY. ALL UNITS ABLE TO RESPOND,*" suddenly comes across the radio dispatch.

The officers drop everything because the call is about the faint shots heard. I am not given a ticket and the officer leaves the money in the trunk of my car. I continue with the run and deliver the money to Tike and Brute. Brute explains to me I was a decoy from the beginning.

"They can't lock you up for having money. Take this for your troubles. This is only a fraction of what we made off this scheme. We intentionally had a snitch tell the police about you were running drugs. While they were focusing on you, Red was running the real stuff to another location. You just brought us the payment." Brute explains while handing me a huge envelope of cash.

"You guys used me?" I respond.

"Homer, all we asked you to do was run for us to pay back your debt. We never discussed what you would transport." Tike adds.

"Shut up, Tike. We do not owe him an explanation. Homer, this is not your life. Your future is too bright. I told you when you started playing football at the schoolyard, you can do something special. I meant it. You should know I will never put you in harm's way just to make a dollar. If this is what you think, then you never valued our friendship. You are pissing me off right now. This is the last time I want to see you in here again." Brute states angrily.

I do not say anything as I place the envelope on the table behind Brute.

"Homer, the money is yours. You are still my boy outside this house. I just do not want to see you in here again." Brute expresses in a calmer tone while facing the opposite direction.

I leave, understanding the message he is trying to get across to me. I intentionally stay low key by spending all my free time with Aimee to avoid any more trouble.

Once I get home, I count the envelope. It is ten thousand dollars in twenty-dollar bills. I quickly hide the money securely behind my dresser. I barely spent the three thousand Brute gave me from winning the city championship and my prom money. I have more than enough money to buy all my supplies for college.

***

Well, this is the end of my first round. I will rate this round as subpar. I made a few birdies, an eagle, and some pars. However, I messed it all up with more bogeys, some detrimental double bogeys, and a few eights on my scorecard. I have made it through some incredible and reprehensible situations from my youth. I hope moving on to the next round is void of discrimination based on my appearance. I am not worried about being labeled an outcast by the Caucasian community. I am worried about the judgment amongst my own people. I have grown up a lot over the last few years.

While flying to Florida for a golf tournament, I finally come to grips with being on outcast. The dictionary defines an outcast as one who is rejected by society. This individual is considered a social misfit in the eyes of others who does not understand the person's circumstances. An outcast is not accepted due to something about the person being different. In my case, my skin color in the wrong environment. I come to the realization I am happy with who I am. I am not a social misfit or a freak of nature. I am me and I am beginning to like myself. I thought looking like this was a curse. Now, I do not care about being anything other than being an outcast. I am thankful for all the good and bad events I experienced. I consider them blessings shaping my mindset and beliefs which will hopefully benefit me as I continue to grow as person. Fortunately, my journey is only getting started and I am excited to find out what is in store for my future.

I grab Aimee's hand while she snuggles in on my shoulder for a quick nap on the plane. I turn to look out the window when the realization surfaces; I haven't dealt with the demons in my head. I need to cast them away because they may cause my rising flame to flicker out quickly.